Why Was Sa...

Biblical Models for Today

M000073106

12 STRONG WOMEN of GOD

MARCI ALBORGHETTI

TWENTY-THIRD PUBLICATIONS

Bayard

185 WILLOW STREET • PO BOX 180 • MYSTIC, CT 06355
TEL: 1-800-321-0411 • FAX: 1-800-572-0788
E-MAIL: ttpubs@aol.com • www.twentythirdpublications.com

Dedication

For God, who joyfully created lively and spirited women.
To Charles, who courageously married one.

In appreciation for the untiring efforts by another group of **Women of God**, I will donate twenty percent of my royalties from this book to the Mothers' Union Sierra Leone Pre-School project. The MU, with more than three million members in over seventy nations, is working to rebuild the Sierra Leone educational infrastructure which has been ravaged by recent wars. I am honored to offer them my small assistance. For more information, please contact me by email at inklin@ntplx.net.

The Scripture passages contained herein are from the *New Revised Standard Version of the Bible*, copyright ©1989, by the Division of Christian Education of the National Council of Churches in the U.S.A. All rights reserved.

Twenty-Third Publications
A Division of Bayard
185 Willow Street
P.O. Box 180
Mystic, CT 06355
(860) 536-2611 or (800) 321-0411
www.twentythirdpublications.com
ISBN:1-58595-326-1

Library of Congress Catalog Card Number: 2004100382
Printed in the U.S.A.

Acknowledgments

This book would be nothing but an intriguing idea were it not for the support and encouragement of Gwen Costello and Mary Carol Kendzia, and I am so grateful to them. Ruby Watrous graciously offered her considerable store of biblical knowledge, and *Twelve Strong Women of God* is a better book thanks to her. My mother's interest in and questions about biblical women gave me a new and welcome perspective.

I am deeply indebted, both spiritually and professionally, to the women in my life who have faced anguish and daunting obstacles with unwavering faith and determination. Among them are Roz Cheney-Mitchell, Julie Comerford, Margaret Crowley, Maria de la Cruz, Phyllis Di Fiore, Anne Kelly-Edmunds, Mary Louise Fennell, Marylin Marino, Sylvie Ann Nucci, Sylvia Modupeh Savage, Dorothy Strelchun, Mary Ann Sullivan, Marion Bond West, and Joni Woelfel.

The women and men in my support group consistently inspire me; they are, simply, my heroes.

Charlie Duffy, my permanent first reader, brought a decidedly fresh perspective to the manuscript and delighted me with his astonished reaction to some of these extraordinary women, particularly Judith.

As always, God nurtures and protects me—often from myself—and remains unfailingly beside me through my own storms. For that, there are no words adequate to express my love and thanks. God knows.

Contents

Introduction

As a child, I was fascinated by my parents' Bible. Though, as was the case then in many Catholic families, we were not big Scripture readers, this bible had lavish illustrations. The stories of Noah, Abraham, Joseph, Moses, David, and, of course, Jesus, were depicted in gorgeously colored pictures; every stunning detail was shown. Before I could even read, before I was even large enough to lift the massive book off the end table where it rested, I was mesmerized by these illustrations. It was only much later, when I actually started reading the Bible regularly, that I realized two things: there were women in the Bible, and their stories were not illustrated. Other than a pitiably reclining Bathsheba, there was not much to go on.

And yet the women of the Bible star in some of its most pivotal and exciting stories. And not just the "back stories," for these women were leaders and warriors in their own right. Judith was stronger and more ruthless than any warrior before or since, just as Abigail was as clever and wise as her second husband, King David. Esther's faith and courage literally saved a nation, just as Deborah's determination galvanized an army.

Indeed, these women may have lived in the past, but they have as much to say to us today as our contemporary leaders. And perhaps more. Who could possibly demonstrate the power of unlikely faith to today's single mother better than Hagar? Who could better speak about the burden of family pain and the need for forgiveness than Miriam? Who could better embody the efficacy of unsolicited charity than the Shunemmitess?

In the coming pages, twelve women from the Old Testament will tell

1

you their stories in their own words. They will shock you, entertain you, educate you, make you laugh, and give you hope. They are the matriarchs and the soldiers of our faith, and their message for us in these confusing and often challenging times could not be fresher or more pertinent. At the end of each story, you will find an active meditation that will help incorporate the story's message into your own life, as well as a series of questions for individual consideration or group discussion.

And finally, the women of my parents' Bible have their own vivid illustrations.

CHAPTER I

Hagar

A single mother's pain and perseverance

GENESIS, CHAPTERS 15—25

When my husband's wife drove my son and me out, she opened a wound that still bleeds today. Though, to be honest, Abram was not really my husband. But after spending over a decade with him, and bearing his first son, I came to think of him as my husband. How else was I to protect my son? How else was I to survive?

If I thought of him as what he really was—a slave owner who forced himself on me at the urging of his wife, Sarai—I would have crumbled under the weight of shame and self-loathing. And I would not crumble. You know him as Abraham and his wife as Sarah, and you probably consider them the first parents of your faith. And so they are. But to me and to the son I bore as a result of Sarai's ambition and Abram's desire, they were something much different.

I was nothing but booty to them at first, a mere Egyptian girl given up as chattel to pacify them as they traveled through our land. Can you imagine my terror as I was ripped from everything and everyone I'd ever known, condemned to wander with these two, whose God I knew only through fear? Indeed, it was fear of their living God—the One, True

God—that prompted the leaders of my people to give me up to them. Our leaders worried that the wrath of this singular God would be stirred if Abram and Sarai were not honored and mollified. And so I became, in a way, an offering to this God for whom my fear later turned to respect and even love.

But at first, at the outset of my banishment to slavery, I did not know him. I was just a child when Abram and Sarai carelessly bound me to their caravan. I was to wait upon Sarai, and she was no easy mistress. Though a great beauty, her spirit was plagued by a barren womb. The fact that she was unable to bear Abram a son—or any child at all—was too heavy a burden for her to bear. So she spread around the weight of that sorrow in her desperation and bitterness. Still, she held Abram's heart captive; he loved none but her while she lived.

From the beginning, there was little I could do to please her. When I dressed her hair, she tore it all loose, claiming I'd done a clumsy job. When I prepared her bread and pottage, she complained that it was watery and lacked spice. As if spices were readily available to those wandering through the desert following a God who'd promised Abram a country and descendants as numerous as the sands of the sea.

Finally Sarai did discover a use for me. When she had utterly despaired of bearing Abram a child, she set in motion a new plan. "My husband will come to you and lie with you, and you will bear the son for us," she told me bluntly one day as I was mending her favorite robe.

I couldn't breathe when I heard these words, and though I knew and feared her magnificent temper, my terror spoke out before good sense could stop it. "Lady, you cannot mean this!" I blurted out, horrified, "I will not do such a thing! I must not!"

Her smooth, lovely brow furrowed, darkening in a way I'd come to dread. Her voice was low and menacing like a storm bearing down on the desert. "You will do whatever I say, because you are mine to command. And since you are my possession, the child you bear will also be mine. It will be born upon my knees, and I will take it from your very body at the moment of birth and present it to my husband as our own child. And you will have nothing to say about it. Our God has decreed that Abram will found a nation, and I am determined that he do so.

Pray you have a son."

I cast about desperately in my mind for a way to escape such a fate. I knew Sarai well enough to realize that she would eventually become jealous of this intimacy with Abram that she now demanded. Nor would she be able to truly love any child I bore as her own, regardless of how ambitious she was to fulfill God's plan. The plain truth was that I was terrified. I'd not been with a man and feared the pain, and now, humiliation that must accompany this scheme. My only hope was that Abram would refuse her plan. Thinking myself clever, I told my mistress, "Surely, Abram's love for you is too deep and wide for him to lie with another."

Her face contorted into a map of conflicting emotions. I saw pride at Abram's devotion war with early signs of the envy I feared, but overriding all was the fierce determination that she should have her way. The same strength that had supported Sarai when she'd decided to leave family and homeland to wander with Abram could become an unbending stubbornness if she felt herself challenged. When she smiled slowly and told me, "Have no worry about my husband for I will persuade him," I knew I was lost.

It took all her machinations and wiles to convince him, but eventually he did, indeed, come to me. To his credit he seemed embarrassed and perhaps because of this, was gentle. Nevertheless, my blood flowed and my pain and shame were great, and as he took me night after night, my fear of Sarai grew into hatred. When I became pregnant, this hatred turned to a contempt that I made little effort to hide. The child growing in me somehow gave me a fiery courage; I thought there was little she could do to hurt me now that she'd gotten her way.

How naive I was! Indeed, at first she treated me gently, offering me the best tidbits of food and a generous amount of goat's milk. As the child took anchor in my womb, I would catch her watching me with a perplexed expression as though she was not sure what she'd wrought. My loathing for her merely grew, and soon her confusion turned to fury when I refused to wait upon her and ignored her attentions. Her ire was stoked by the kind attention Abram now paid me. He who'd taken no notice of me before, now brought me small gifts and urged me to rest, particularly in the heat of the day.

The explosion was inevitable, and only in its burning heat did I realize how I'd miscalculated. To escape Sarai's unbounded anger, Abram gave her leave to treat me as she pleased, and she began to abuse me in every way. She berated me continually, often slapping me and driving me to labor harder than ever before. But she was careful in her rage, never beating me in such a way as to harm the child and forcing me to eat more than my portion even when I was too sick or exhausted to want food.

My body and soul cried out against such cruelty. It was all too much. In the same time period that my body was changing in ways I'd not imagined, I had risen from the base level of slave to the status of wife, and now I was being cast back unto the lowest place. I wept unceasingly, and that alone seemed to give her some pleasure, though Abram couldn't bear to look at me.

In the end I ran away, heading into the desert though I had not money or food or resources. Yet I had no wish to die; indeed I'd no plan at all other than to escape my mistress. I'd not traveled a day's span, before God's voice found me in the hot sand. I'd learned nothing but fear for this God of Abram and Sarai, and so when he told me to return and subject myself to Sarai, my heart cried out in anguish. I dared not oppose him—who was I, after all? Still, I could not but wonder what kind of God would want to see me so ill-used. Didn't he understand what would become of me, of my son, in Sarai's home? Why had he allowed this terrible plan to come into Sarai's heart? Did he wish to see my pain? Was his love reserved only for Abram and Sarai, with none left for the likes of me and my son?

I spoke none of these words aloud, and yet God hears. He spoke in a clear voice, assuring me that my son—whom I must name Ishmael, or "God hears"—would father nations. All that was left to me was to trust. Against all reason—for what is reason in the eyes of God?—my heart was lightened, and I turned immediately around and went back. With every step my confidence increased as I realized that the God of Abram and Sarai was now the God of Hagar and her son as well.

They were waiting when I returned, and Sarai was all for punishing me severely. But Abram looked closely at me, and I wonder to this very day if he saw the signs of God's favor in my aspect. I think he might have for he administered a rare rebuke to Sarai and merely told me to have some supper and go to sleep.

From that time forward, there was an uneasy truce between Sarai and me, though in truth, the unease was all hers. I carried God's promise close to my heart, feeling nothing could harm me now that he'd spoken to me. I realized of course that Abram had warned his wife against harming me, perhaps even telling her his suspicion that I'd been touched by God. Whatever the reason, Sarai did me no more harm; and when Ishmael was born, I did indeed deliver him unto her waiting arms. As she carried him from the birthing tent with nary a backward glance at me, I felt a deep foreboding that only the memory of God's assurances could silence.

Years passed and, as I'd expected, Sarai soon wanted little to do with me and my son. He was acknowledged by his father as heir, and God even changed the names of Abram and Sarai to confirm his promise to them. But Sarai's anguish at her sterile womb plagued her into old age, and she did not take the pleasure in Ishmael that she might have. Abram loved my boy, however, and treated him as a son. Soon after God's affirmation, Abram took Ishmael and all the men of our community and circumcised them as a sign to the Lord God. My son was thirteen years old when he received at the hand of his father the mark of God. Ishmael was a strong, handsome, able boy, and I could barely conceal my loving pride on this auspicious day. Sarai did not join the rejoicing.

But within two short years, she did rejoice and her joy signaled the end of my contentment. God visited Abram and Sarai in the guise of angel-men, and promised that Sarai would bear a son within a year. Sarai, not knowing that it was God Who spoke—though I did—smirked bitterly at these words. Despite her doubt and her century of life, she did bear a son and named him Isaac. She took to her bed at the first sign of pregnancy, and I was forced to wait on her hand and foot for the duration. She was not a little smug, but I was beyond taking offense at her. God had freed me from such pettiness, yet I worried constantly for my son. I knew that my mistress, who grew thick in the waist as she lay abed day after day, would never tolerate my son in proximity to hers.

So it was. Soon after the infant Isaac was born, she began once again to look upon me and my son with extreme disfavor. Her envy grew as Isaac and Ishmael became close as brothers will, and her distress increased as Abram looked upon his two sons with equal love. After all, it was known by now that God had promised to found nations upon both boys, and Abram was content to await the fulfillment of such a generous commitment.

Sarai, however, was not. She wanted every and all blessings to come only to Isaac, and often I would observe her watching Ishmael with something akin to hatred in her eyes. Ishmael often took care of his little brother, and this kindness only served to more deeply draw her ire. The very sight of the two boys together could infuriate her, as if Ishmael would steal Isaac's birthright before her very eyes.

Soon, all our people could hear her angry voice in Abram's tent, criticizing Ishmael and demanding that he not be allowed to usurp her Isaac. She had forgotten her insistence, over sixteen years earlier, that I bear her and Abram a "son." Now that very "son" was anathema to her, and she cried out to her husband day and night that Ishmael must go. Abram at first ignored her, dismissing her fears as foolish, but Sarai was relentless and, as always, her husband could not withstand her onslaught.

Abram came to me one morning, and I could read the future in his drawn, mournful face. He wordlessly handed me some small provisions to take into the harsh desert, and then he kissed an uncomprehending Ishmael who in turn embraced his father heartily, sensing he needed comfort but not knowing why. Abram turned away without speaking.

I bade my son follow me and together we walked out into the same desert I'd fled to years before. Then, I carried him in my womb; now he strode innocently by my side. As we left I noticed how the tents slowly emptied until every member of our caravan stood watching. Tears streamed down the faces of many women and children and not a few of the strong men. Ishmael had been a cheerful boy, much beloved by the people, upon whom our hopes had been placed for many years. Now the people grieved what they knew to be our certain death—for who could survive banishment to the unforgiving desert? Yet no one dared speak against Sarai. She and Isaac were nowhere to be seen; she'd even denied the brothers a parting kiss.

I could not bear to tell Ishmael that we'd been exiled, and that to a likely death, so I told him his father had sent us on a journey. When he asked our destination, I spoke half-bitterly, "To God." My son, an obedient, affable boy, accepted this.

But I could not accept it! "Why?" I cried silently to God. "Is this—this shameful death—the consummation of your promise?! That my son should die in an agony of thirst and exhaustion while I watch? Is Sarai better than I that her dreams come true while mine wither and die in this scorching heat? I've named my son for you, and do you now refuse to hear?" God made me no answer.

Too soon our water and food were gone. We struggled on as long as we could until we finally collapsed in the burning sand. Ishmael looked askance at me as if to ask, "Mother what have you done to us? Surely my father, Abram, did not intend such an end to our journey?" Yet Abram did. But I still could not bring myself to tell this truth to my son. And so, consumed with stinging grief and exhaustion, I laid him gently under some scrawny brush that provided the only meager shade I could find. I moved some distance away from him, casting myself onto the ground and vowing I would not watch my son die. There I lay, weeping and waiting for slow death.

But we did not die. God had not forgotten his promise to a homeless, pregnant slave girl those many years before, and now he roused me in the guise of an angel, asking, "What troubles you, Hagar?" And when I was too dumbfounded to answer, the voice continued, "Do not be afraid; for God has heard the voice of the boy. Come and lift your son and hold him fast for I will make a great nation of him." I opened my eyes then, and God showed me a well of water that had sprung up there in the desert. I gave Ishmael to drink and took the water myself, amazed at how it revitalized and nourished us. I filled our water skin with the blessed water and we continued on.

We eventually settled in the wilderness of Paran, living among the nomads who, though wild and sometimes brutal, treated us well enough. My son grew into a man himself among such men and took on their ways, though he never lost faith in our God, the God of Abram, the God of Isaac and, for us, the God of Hagar and Ishmael.

Despite this seeming bond, we would never again live among the people of Abram and Sarai. My son indeed founded a nation, but it was not a nation of Hebrews. I was determined to find a wife for him from my own people, and when the time came for him to marry, I sent to Egypt for his first bride. I know it was wrong, but I took great pleasure in knowing that Abram's son would marry into the people from whom his mother was taken by force. The former slave girl would be mother-in-law to the future queen of a nation. God forgive my pride, but the very thought of this delighted me!

I also lived to see another day of vindication, though I've finally learned that vengeance should not be the desire of men and women, when Ishmael gave his daughter, my granddaughter, as wife to Isaac's renegade son Esau. I fancied that Esau was much like my Ishmael, the firstborn son who was rejected by his mother, Rebekah, in favor of the second son she most loved. More subtle than her mother-in-law Sarai, Rebekah used deceit and wiles instead of shrieks and demands to have her way, but in the end she achieved the same end as Sarai: the banishment to the wilderness of one son to preserve and elevate the other. She tricked Isaac into giving Esau's birthright to her beloved Jacob, while Esau fled to the desert in shame and wild grief. Like his uncle, my son, Ishmael, Esau became a powerful nomad, and I was inordinately pleased when he took my beautiful granddaughter, Mahalath, to wife. I confess I spent not a little time exulting in the thought of how Abram, Sarai, and Rebekah would react to this half-Egyptian choice of a bride!

God fulfilled his promise to me, and I lived to regret my bitter words and thoughts of despair. That he forgave me and blessed Ishmael despite my doubt is some measure of his greatness. Ishmael did become the patriarch of a great nation; indeed even the Hebrew books calls his twelve sons "princes according to their tribes," just as Jacob's twelve sons became the princes of Israel. Our tribes settled in what is now called the Sinai Peninsula, not so very far from the nations of Israel.

And yet the rift that was rent by Sarai—and yes, I now know, widened by my pride and unforgiving nature—never healed. You and your world live with the consequences of our faithlessness and envy each day. I sometimes wonder how the three great nations of faith, now numbering in the billions, that sprang from Abram have caused each other so much pain and devastation. And then I remember.

Active Meditation

Hagar's perseverance and faith in the God who "adopted" her kept her and Ishmael alive against impossible odds. Desperate in a way that many single and/or abandoned mothers might easily understand, Hagar mustered up enough strength to do one thing: listen to God. Besieged by a world that often delivers uncertainty, danger, fear, and even the kind of grief that only a mother can feel, are we able to trust the seemingly unlikely and sometimes incomprehensible direction of God?

Sometimes it seems almost impossible to trust with our whole hearts and souls. especially when our children are involved. And yet, we can take small steps toward utter trust in God. When we feel disappointed and exhausted, we can listen for God's soft voice. When we are hungry and thirsty, we can contribute time and/or money to a food bank or homeless shelter to help the Hagar of today. When we think we can't bear to watch our child on a path that seems destructive, we can make yet another effort to reach out to him or her. When we feel completely betrayed by those who have seemed close to us and want nothing more than to reject humanity as a whole, we can seek new friends, new communities, new hope.

Reflection/Discussion Questions

1. How does Hagar's experience as a shunned single mother mirror the plight of today's impoverished and/or abandoned women?
2. Have you ever dismissed or ignored a single mother or abandoned woman without fully exploring or understanding her circumstances?
3. Would you consider raising a child on your own?
4. Can you identify a situation in your own life when you felt betrayed, banished and/or cruelly used? Were you able to turn completely in trust to God?
5. How has the conflict between Sarah and Hagar played out over the centuries to reflect today's Middle East?

CHAPTER II

Pharaoh's Daughter

Love that freed a nation

EXODUS, CHAPTER 2

I detested my father. Not that he would ever have noticed. I was, after all, one of many children he'd fathered with his wives and concubines; there were scores of us, all arranged in order according to how he favored our mothers. The wives, of course, were automatically accorded more status than the concubines, though I think he preferred his concubines. They were probably a relief to him, not clamoring incessantly as his wives did for material and political demonstrations of his favor.

The wives, often brutally competitive, mostly sought these symbols for their children. The more attention and gifts showered upon the child, the more status accorded the mother. Naturally, then, wives who'd borne my father sons were the most powerful, and the most competitive. Among them, this vying for my father's attention, was often severe enough to become menacing; it was not unknown for the mother of one prince to plot violence against another son, or even against another mother currying favor for her young princeling. But such events were kept from my father. He abhorred discord among his teeming family, and was swift to punish.

My mother, then, had her hands full. Oh, it was not that she had a prince to champion or even protect; I was the only child Pharaoh had given her. Yet she was a wife and a great favorite of his, probably for her gentle—weak, by my way of thinking—demeanor and undemanding nature. No, my mother's big problem was me. Because she was a beloved wife, we were much envied by the others, who watched carefully for any mischief or disobedience they might report to my father.

I gave them plenty to observe, to my poor mother's great and continual consternation. Perhaps because I was an only child, thrust into this massive network of women and children, I never managed to fit in. Even as a child, I refused to join in the girls' games, desiring instead to chase after the boys and join their rougher play. While my many half-sisters learned to please our father—and thus, their own mothers—by producing beautifully stitched tapestries and savory dishes, I begged to be allowed to hunt and fish with the boys. I cared not one whit about pleasing my father—with either cooking or hunting skills—but I sought the freedom afforded the princelings, my half-brothers. I yearned to be allowed to run freely, to explore the riverbanks, to learn the arts of warfare and battle, to study the scrolls.

Needless to say, this was much remarked upon by the other wives and concubines. I imagine they made my mother, who could barely control me, miserable with their snide comments and ridicule. My mother had not the energy or the temperament to truly discipline me, and they viciously mocked what half-hearted efforts she made. Had she been less popular with my father, they would have simply dismissed me as an odd child undeserving of attention. But because Pharaoh loved my mother, and therefore indulged me, they kept sharp watch upon us, seeking a way to diminish my mother in my father's eyes. Even the wives with sons feared my mother's influence with Pharaoh, particularly because she was still young enough to bear more children. Pharaoh made no attempt to conceal his love for her, or his desire that she give him a son. It was an unspoken, but well-accepted, fact that any son borne him by my mother would be highly favored.

So my mother was a threat to all the wives, and I, they hoped, would be her downfall. They were constantly running to the high household slaves, the men who had my father's ear, to report my antics.

"She returned home covered with the mud of the Nile when she should have been working her needle."

"She cannot even make a simple pottage of lentils or grind meal."

"She teases her sisters and frightens them when they try to join her play."

"She ignores her mother's poor attempts at discipline and mocks the instruction of other, wiser wives."

"She shouts and runs with the boys as though she fancies herself a princeling."

Of course it was this last accusation that most terrified them; they feared that if I sought to join the princelings, my father might actually start treating me as such. They needn't have worried. My father was too narrow-minded and short-sighted for such thinking. No daughter in his household would ever be more than an ornament and companion to him and her brothers. I knew that, and disdained my father for it. He was to me, a small-minded, stubborn man; and yet I knew it was thanks to him that I enjoyed a freedom that shocked and aggravated his other wives. And I took pleasure in this.

For it seemed the more outrageous my demeanor, the more my father simply laughed and indulged me. That my behavior kept my mother on tenterhooks, lest her enemies succeed in using me to drive a wedge between her and Pharaoh, bothered me not at all. As I grew out of childhood, my scorn for my father and this treacherous extended family grew into a sort of rebellion; the type that only a girl-woman can fully understand. It seemed to me that everything about my father, his household, and his governing was wrong. I resented his power over me, and yes, over my mother, who spent her life waiting for just a word or two from his pouting lips. I thought him a hypocrite, taking money and goods from his subjects in order to better spoil his many children, wives, and concubines. I grew disgusted at the riches and excess that cluttered our lives, especially when I walked the streets and saw the poverty of my fellow Egyptians.

But what appalled me the most, what made me come to hate my father with my whole heart, was his treatment of the slaves. The Hebrews had been subjugated and were treated as a slave class, forced to take upon themselves the most appalling and brutal of tasks. It was they who bore the back-breaking, spirit-crushing, burden of constructing my father's monuments and official buildings. Not only were they forced to perform the tedious bodily labor, they were assigned the painstaking job of actually mixing and making every single brick. Can anyone in your world imagine how difficult and massive a task this was? How time-consuming and wearying?

And add to such travail that this was no labor of love for the Hebrews. They were not making and laying bricks for their own homes, their own temples, their own altars to their God. No. They were slaves! This proud people with their own God, their Yahweh, their own heritage, their own culture, were forced to perform such demeaning labor for their captors. I would watch them trudge back and forth from their work, just imagining how they must hate us. We were everything they abhorred. We ignored their Yahweh, instead worshipping many deities, indeed, making a mere man into a god. It was not lost on me that my father, the man I thought least worthy to be so elevated, was the "god" of my people. He was hardly a responsible father to all his progeny, how could he be a god?

Knowing this only increased my sorrow for the Hebrews. At first, they hardly acknowledged me as I spent more and more time observing them. By the age of fourteen, I spent all my free time, all the time I could escape from those who watched me so closely, studying them. I was most drawn to the children, and they were the ones who most often gazed back at me, curious as to why Pharaoh's daughter watched them. Yet they did not fear or fawn over me as any Egyptian would have. They had a dignity—both the children and the adults—with which they bore their servitude. It was as though slavery could not diminish them, as though freedom would surely come.

This puzzled me. No Egyptian commoner would dare meet my eyes. I was the daughter of Pharaoh! And though it seemed nothing but an encumbrance to me, my people feared to offend me in any way. The punishment for those who did would be swift and severe. And so I was a solitary stranger among my own people: despised and scorned by the children and women of my father's household, and feared by common Egyptians. Yet the Hebrews were not afraid of me, nor, I came to suspect, did they particularly respect me. It was as though they considered me no greater than they, as though nothing in my status or demeanor could subjugate their spirit. I saw this in the eyes of the children, and eventually, those adults who began to take notice of me. This boldness only increased my fascination with such a people.

I soon came to realize two things about the Hebrews. First, they worshiped and depended only upon their God, and so my place as an Egyptian princess meant nothing to them, nor did they recognize my father as even a minor deity. In that, I heartily agreed with them. The second thing that attracted me to them was the importance they put on the bond of family. Unlike the slaves I'd seen in the past, where every individual sought his or her own survival, these people would not countenance the separation of families. They were fierce in their determination to stay together. All children were cherished, and the culture of the Hebrew family grew strong in Egypt.

In fact, it was that very strength that drew my father's rage, though in truth it was his fear that made him oppress the Hebrews. Their quiet dignity and growing presence in Egypt terrified him. His predecessor had welcomed the Jews, placing much trust in the wisdom and household of the Hebrew slave Joseph. It had been Joseph who had saved Egypt from starvation and ruin in the time of famine. Because that Pharaoh had loved Joseph, the Jews in Egypt, though still slaves, had been allowed and even encouraged to flourish. By the time my father took the throne of Pharaoh, the Hebrews were thought to be more numerous in the land than Egyptians, and my father—who was far more venal and dull-witted than his predecessor—saw the Hebrews as a threat. Their devotion to Yahweh only infuriated him the more for they simply refused to worship anyone but their God—including Pharaoh! Thus it was my father who multiplied the oppression and abuse of the Hebrews in a way unknown for generations. But as I saw every day in my observations, the Jews merely grew stronger and more committed to Yahweh and their families.

Late one day, as I watched the Hebrew slaves return from their long day of labor, an Egyptian slave driver cuffed a young Hebrew boy, and when the boy fell, the man moved forward to beat him. The slave driver had not seen me, and I started forward in a rage, fully prepared now to use the full measure of the power I so disdained to punish the man. But I'd barely taken a step or drawn breath before the boy's father stepped between his son and the slave driver. I was stunned by such foolish courage; the slave driver would now first beat the father senseless and then start on the boy. Not only was the Hebrew unarmed, his clothes were worn by work and heat and he had no head covering, not even a shawl to protect himself with. Even as I recovered myself and prepared to intervene, an astonishing thing happened. The slave driver raised his cord to slice the father's face to shreds. And then stopped. I could not see what it was he saw in the face of that Hebrew man, but gradually his heavily muscled arm, glistening with oil, dropped. Looking away from the eyes of the Hebrew, he laughed rudely and muttered a curse. But he also stepped back. The father bent to lift his son gently, and the family continued on their way home.

It was at that moment, I now realize, that my future was decided.

I was fifteen when I found the boy. I had gone to bathe in the Nile, more because I was hot with anger and disgust than because I needed to wash. I had just finished one of endless arguments with my mother over the fate of the Hebrews. You see, my father, in his wrath, had ordered that all Hebrew boys were to be killed at birth and thrown into the Nile! This was his brilliant, compassionate solution to the "problem" of the Hebrew multitude in Egypt! My father, Pharaoh, the craven idiot! Murderer! At first the fool had tried to force the Hebrew midwives to kill the babes as they emerged from the womb, but those God-fearing, family-loving women had thwarted him with lies and deception. Not to be denied his cruel power, he decreed that all Egyptians should drown every boy born to a Hebrew woman.

I was sickened. I could not sleep or eat. I cursed his blood that ran in my veins. My mother was no better in my eyes. I relentlessly demanded that she use her wiles to prevail upon my father to withdraw the decree. I hounded her, making no secret of my angry plea and threatening to go to Pharaoh myself. The louder and more desperate I grew in my pursuit of her, the more she cringed away. She knew that our enemies in Pharaoh's palace were gleefully noting my subterfuge and, doubtless, reporting it to my father's obsequious henchmen. I didn't care. Let them hear me! They disgusted me as much as my mother did. How could anyone countenance such savagery?

My mother took to concealing herself from me whenever possible. In her fear of my outbursts and her abiding desire only for self-preservation and my father's favor, she utterly refused to hear me. It was after another such maddening encounter that I strode out to plunge into the river, trailed as always by the mute, resentful maids assigned to this most difficult and dangerous of Pharaoh's daughters. They also wearied me, and I waded into the water, keeping myself at as great a distance from them as possible.

It was then that I saw the basket.

It was upriver from me, and I imperiously ordered one of the youngest maids to fetch it. Pulling a face that made her displeasure clear, she angrily hiked up her robe and stumbled into the reeds, acting as though I'd ordered her into a cobra pit. She finally managed to snag the basket, and brought it to me, whimpering as if she'd been beaten with cords. Not deigning to acknowledge her whining, I snatched the basket from her, surprised at its sudden weight. Shielding it from the maids with my body, I opened the carefully constructed vessel, and after one swift glance, slammed it closed again and turned to my maids. In my most commanding voice, I dismissed them, telling them I wished to be alone and that they might have the rest of the day free to tarry at the bazaar. What curiosity they might have had about the contents of the basket evaporated at the prospect of such wanton freedom, and they fled, not daring to look back lest I come to my senses.

I settled myself on the river bank, finding a spot well-concealed from any who might pass by. Gingerly I opened the basket again, half-fearful that what I'd seen was merely a vision and that it would be empty. It was not. The babe stared back at me, his dark eyes wide and fathomless. He bore the mark of the Hebrews, and couldn't have been more than four months old. He seemed to watch me solemnly, as though interested to see what I might do next. I could hardly catch my breath, and at his somber gaze, I released a sound between a sob and laughter.

Immediately I heard rustling nearby. Frightened at the prospect of discovery and enraged that one of the maids had disobeyed, I swung around, ready to lash out mercilessly. A small girl crept forward from her hiding place in the rushes, not more than a few cubits away. She was a Hebrew, her clothes were threadbare, and she met my gaze with that odd dignity I'd come to recognize. Still, I feared her intent and demanded coldly, "What are you doing lurking about here, girl?"

Brazenly ignoring my query, she replied with the question she'd rehearsed, "Do you wish a nurse for the child, princess?"

Her question took me aback, but my stunned mind had recovered and was working rapidly. The girl had been sent to watch the fate of the babe in the basket, probably by his mother. Indeed, the girl might well be the infant's sister or perhaps a cousin. I realized instantly that the "nurse" she would fetch, were I to give assent, would be the babe's own mother.

I gave it.

They returned so rapidly I knew they must live nearby, but I'd had enough time to work out my plan. The woman who accompanied the child was thin and haggard, but her face lit with joy at the sight of the babe. She remained silent, staring at me in mute appeal. I spoke rapidly, telling her to take and nurse the babe, but that she must return him to me when he was weaned. Her face fell at this last instruction, but I insisted impatiently, "There is no other way for him to survive!"

I had not yet allowed myself to think that I would not survive without him. After just these few moments, my bitter shrunken heart had expanded and filled with a love so heavy it was overwhelming. I thrust the basket rapidly at her, telling myself I feared discovery, but knowing if I held him another moment, I would not let him go.

No sooner had I sent them away, then I called them back. "Take this," I said, yanking the ring of Pharaoh's house off my finger, "If anyone should threaten the child before you return him, show him this and say that he is under Pharaoh's protection." I smiled to myself, knowing full well that no one in my father's household would be surprised when the reprobate princess announced she'd lost her seal ring. As the woman turned again to go, I called to her, "And send the girl here to meet me upon occasion to tell me how the boy does." Her eyes flickered at this, and I added brutally, "If you thwart me in any of this, I will see your whole household destroyed. I am your only chance to save this boy and everything you cherish." She glanced away, her face darkening, but she took the ring as I bid her and slipped away through the reeds until she had disappeared with her daughter. And my son.

Such is how I thought of him from that moment on. And I thought of nothing but him. Moses. That was the name he was given, the girl reported to me during one of our meetings. True to her word, the mother sent her often to speak with me, and I hungered after every word of my son. Both the girl and her mother seemed resigned to the fact that I would soon have the boy; after all, I was Pharaoh's daughter: I might have whatever I wished. And I was ravenous for the redemption that being mother to this boy would bring me.

For that is how I came to think of this: that the God of the Hebrews had given me the chance to save this one boy and so to redeem myself from the filth of my father's brutal sins. I did not let myself consider the pain I would cause his mother and family, reasoning instead that I had saved him and that they should be grateful. Which was all very true, but as I know now, not very kind.

During the three long years of waiting, I prepared carefully for the coming of Moses. I recreated myself, or so it was said among the vicious, and doubtless disappointed, members of my father's household. Though I had long scorned my mother's abject weakness and wily dependence on my father, I now modeled myself after her. I fawned over Pharaoh, playing the repentant daughter determined to show my gratitude for all I'd been given. I feigned sorrow for my previous rebellious behavior, blaming it on childishness and ignorance. Biting my tongue, I praised my corrupt father to all who would listen, much to the dismay of those in our household who hoped to see me disgraced. I even courted these, my enemies, letting them believe I'd transformed myself into the perfect, obedient princess. I was determined to completely win Pharaoh's favor and to make certain that no one would have an ill word to speak of me. If I must turn myself into a simpering, sweet-tempered fool to protect my son, so be it.

For, indeed, I intended to bring Moses into Pharaoh's house as just that: my son. I had many long months to craft my story, and I lingered lovingly over the task. For nearly three years, all I could do was prepare, and I did it well. On the day I had appointed during one of my secret meetings with Moses' sister, I dismissed my maids and set out alone. I met my son and his mother at the bend in the Nile where I'd first found him. It was my first sight of him in nearly three years, and it took my breath away. Though she carried him, I could see he was big enough to walk, and indeed, squirmed in her arms to escape. He was a strong, sturdy boy, with a set to his chin already that was stubborn and willful. And yet those same beautiful eyes fixed on me with lively curiosity, just as they had so many months ago. I devoured him with my eyes, I'd hungered and thirsted for this moment for so long.

His mother's face, wizened and ruined by the sun though she had no more than thirty years, was covered with tears, and the sister sobbed aloud. Ignoring them effortlessly—for, after all, I was the child's only chance at survival; I was his real mother—I commanded, "Put the boy down."

Shaking with wordless sobs, she slowly obeyed me. I crouched down and held open my arms, and just as I'd dreamed every night for three years, he ran into them. Of course, what three-year-old wouldn't be fascinated by the glimmering gold bracelets that circled my arms, the jewels in my ears and hair, the silver collar that glowed around my throat, the black kohl that circled my eyes, the bright rouge on my lips? His drab, crone-like mother never stood a chance.

Stripping off his rags, I quickly dressed him in the garb of an Egyptian boy, having secretly purchased the clothes at the bazaar. The mother watched dully, knowing any intervention would be futile, but his sister, who was more accustomed to me, cried out, "My brother is a Levite! He is to be a priest!"

Lifting Moses in my arms, I looked at them coldly. "Priest?" I spoke dismissively. "My son will be a prince!" And then I bore him away, not looking back even when the woman's single wail rent the air. Moses stiffened in my grasp at the sound, but I murmured softly to him and gently turned his face into my scented shoulder.

Thinking on it now, I cannot imagine what cruelty possessed me. I thought myself a mother at that moment. I had no concept of the agony a real mother feels. Seventeen years later, that anguish became my life and remained with me forever.

But that day, I brought Moses into my father's household, claiming that I'd found this young Egyptian boy wandering alone through the reeds of the Nile. "No woman who lets a child roam free in such a dangerous place is worthy of motherhood," I declared indignantly, and then announced that I would raise the boy myself to be a true Egyptian. Three years before I would have been laughed out of the palace, but I'd done a careful job of convincing everyone I'd changed. I was no longer the wild, discordant girl who could not be controlled. I was now a demure, gentle-natured princess who had earned the abundant favor of her father.

No one, then, dared gainsay me.

Except Moses. For despite my best efforts, he never lost a sense of the heritage he'd been born to; I tried to raise him as an Egyptian prince, but he indeed remained the Levite priest. And the shrieked prophecy of his sister rang in my ears as he grew more distant from me with each passing year. Was it a judgment upon me that his initial adoration of me gradually became a simmering resentment? Was it my punishment that he came to hate the trappings of Pharaoh's palace as much as I had at his age? Were the coals heaped upon my aging head no more than the weight of his scorn?

Inevitably, reports of his rebellion made their way to my father's court. Just as the enemies of my mother had used me against her, so did those who envied me my father's favor, use Moses against me. At first Pharaoh heard my pleas that he was just a boy who didn't know what he was doing. But when my son murdered an Egyptian who was abusing a Hebrew—just as two decades before, I might have had the slave driver who beat the Hebrew boy put to death—Pharaoh could tolerate no more.

He ordered my son—"the bastard son," evil whispers now echoed through the palace—arrested. And so that very night, feeling a sabre had ripped me asunder, I pressed a fortune in gold and jewels upon Moses and sent him away. As I stood sobbing, he strode away wordlessly, not turning back except to fling the sack of treasures at my feet. I was not much older than his mother had been seventeen years before when I'd borne her son away without a single backward glance.

Later I learned that he had foolishly remained in the region until someone, a Hebrew as it turned out, taunted him for having killed the

Egyptian. My poor son, knowing then that even his own people would not accept him, fled.

Barren and alone, I grew old in Pharaoh's palace. Though still beautiful, I would take no man. The stubborn, intractable girl who'd been the talk of the court became its pathetic, muttering joke in her old age. Was I comforted by hearing of the man my son became? I was comforted to know that he lived, and finally in the role he alone could choose, flourished.

But could I take pride in him? No. I was too aware by then of how poorly I'd served him and his family. His success was not because of me, but despite me. That knowledge, coupled with my own grief, pierced me more deeply every day until I felt I must be leaving a trail of black blood wherever I went.

Yet I loved him every day of my life, and every night when I closed my eyes, I saw only his own beautiful, brilliant eyes staring up at me from the basket in the reeds.

Active Meditation

As we see with Moses and his two mothers, the bond between parent and child can be, at once, self-sacrificing and selfish. Mothers must sacrifice their very selves in order to give birth and raise a child. And quite naturally, most mothers expect and hope for something back, if only their child's unconditional love and respect. Whether we are in the role of child or parent, each of us is probably both self-sacrificing and self-serving.

As we imagine the regrets that both Moses' mothers must have felt, let's also consider the regrets we might feel if we embraced unhealthy patterns in our own families. If we are clinging to a role or attitude that is self-serving at the expense of a parent or child, what might we do to change? Is it a matter of discussing a conflict? Admitting a fault? Confessing a weakness? Surrendering a complaint or grudge to God? Forgiving? Accepting forgiveness?

If we identify and implement steps to change selfish behavior now—regardless of our role in the family—we may avoid bitter recriminations and piercing sorrow later.

Reflection/Discussion Questions

1. Moses is seen by some as the precursor to Christ in that both came to save the Jews and sacrificed themselves in the process. Do you see similarities between Pharaoh's daughter and Mary, mother of Jesus? What about between Moses' mother and Mary?

2. Pharaoh persecuted the Jews because he feared their strength in both numbers and faith. Do you believe that anti-Semitism today is also motivated by fear?

3. If you are a parent, can you identify ways in which you are both self-sacrificing and selfish? How about in your role as a child?

4. Do you believe that your parents struck a balance between self-sacrificing and selfish?

5. Today, we sometimes hear of conflicts between adoptive parents and biological parents who later decide to try to regain custody of the child. Do you believe it is noble to give up a child because the adopting parents appear more capable of caring for that child?

CHAPTER III

Miriam

God's healing power over envy's poison

EXODUS, CHAPTERS 2—15, 32; NUMBERS, CHAPTER 12

Naked and alone in my tent—a tent now set shamefully apart from my family and people—I drew a deep breath and looked at my ruined body. The terrifyingly ugly signs of leprosy were everywhere, marking my skin with lesions and even running sores. Horrified when I saw what I knew I would, I moaned at the devastation. The humiliation! The punishment! The crushing of my body and soul!

How had I come to such a pass?

Unable to bear the sight, I drew the rough robe—so different from the soft robes of power I'd grown accustomed to—over myself, and closed my eyes. An unexpected sleep stole over me, and with it, the dream. Or perhaps I should say, the memory.

My skin was flawless and supple, as pure as my young soul. I waited, a mere child hiding in the rushes, my eyes fixed on the precious basket. My mother had set it, with its cherished contents, on the bank of the Nile. With tears staining her own face, aged by worry and work, she bid me follow its progress and bring her back word of its end. I sobbed too, for the basket held my infant brother, and we both knew what that end must be.

25

Death, whether by drowning in the violent arms of the river, or by the stinging bite of its deadly vipers, or even by the fate my mother vainly hoped to avoid: murder at the hand of any Egyptian who found him.

For that had been the decree of Pharaoh: that every boy born of a Hebrew woman must die, preferably drowned in the Nile, the river much revered and worshiped by the heathen Egyptians. We Jews had no recourse; we were a slave nation, homeless and now closely oppressed by this cruel Pharaoh. His vicious repression had stunned us. Though we'd long been displaced to Egypt, the Pharaoh before this one had treated us with some respect, loving as he did, our patriarch, Joseph. Although Joseph had been sold into Egypt as a boy-slave, he'd won the attention and, eventually, affection of that Pharaoh. Thus, we'd enjoyed freedom to worship and flourish as a people, though we pined for a homeland.

All that had changed when this venal, arrogant Pharaoh assumed the throne. He had no use for the Hebrew nation—not our achievements or our counsel. Instead, he feared our numbers and success, soon coming to hate us. Oppression followed, and when even that could not force us to worship him as he demanded, or to abandon our beloved Yahweh, he ordered all our boy infants to be killed.

My mother, who had borne many daughters but only one other son, my brother Aaron, years before Pharaoh's heartless decree, was torn with the grief that this new son would be so sacrificed. In the three months that she kept him hidden, her anguish intensified, for my brother was an extraordinary infant. He never wailed or carried on, as my mother frequently assured the rest of us we had, nor did he sleep as oft as most babes. He seemed possessed of a quiet brilliance, if such a thing may be said of an infant, and contented himself with observing all that went on around him. To my thinking, he was more like a wizened old man than a babe, but my mother loved his sweet silence and studious gaze. She was driven near mad at the thought that he would be ripped from her arms and thrown into the Nile like a rag.

My father, too heartbroken himself to make her hear reason, soon succumbed to her desperate plan. While she watched closely over his shoulder, he constructed this sturdy basket of papyrus, bitumen, and pitch, and lined it with the finest linen of our household—a scrap of cloth lovingly preserved from their wedding in happier times. Though it would go into the river, the first drops of water christening that basket were my father's tears. A Levite of the priestly class, my father suffered greatly at the suppression of our religion. More than the undignified, brutal labor he was forced to undertake; more than the enslavement of our people; more than our expulsion from our home; more than the humiliation of his wife and children, he agonized over the loss of our rituals and what he increasingly feared to be the anger of Yahweh. To my father, Pharaoh's decree that boy infants be drowned was further confirmation of his dreaded suspicion.

And now his very own wife had gone mad with love of this babe, willing to risk the lives of her other son and daughters and her husband to defy the Egyptians. My father, having finished the basket as she demanded, dropped his weary head into his hands as my mother snatched up the vessel and took it to where the babe lay. She raised him in her arms, holding him up for a lingering inspection as if she would memorize every feature, and then as we all watched sorrowfully, placed him softly into the basket. She gazed so long upon him, and he did indeed stare back as was his wont, that I thought she might not secure the cover. But with a sudden groan, she grasped the cover and pressed it tightly over the basket.

Even then, the boy did not utter a sound.

My mother hefted the basket and turned to us defiantly. My father made no attempt to even lift his face, much less meet her eyes. My brother Aaron, now a young man, watched her for a moment and then turned away abruptly and strode out. Though at seven years, I was but half his age, I felt a sudden pang for Aaron. How must it feel to be the eldest son, born and grown before Pharaoh's vile decree, and yet so discounted and seemingly unloved by his mother? The strange and tiny babe had far surpassed him in her regard. She did not notice that Aaron had gone out.

At that moment my heart knit itself to Aaron's, and I felt his bitter betrayal as completely as if it were my own.

My mother went out, bidding me follow. We traveled some distance along the river before she stopped abruptly in the reeds and rushes. Pharaoh's palace was visible from where we stood, and I was a little frightened to be so near the monster who had caused this tragedy. My mother, her face now wet with tears gone unshed for so long, told me to watch and see what would befall the babe. She hurried away, not looking back or even brushing the hair from my face, the one token of affection I'd come to expect from her.

I felt afraid and abandoned, and as hours passed and the hot sun rose high, filled with a fierce resentment. Aaron was not the only one my mother had cast away in her insanity! Why must I wait here for certain disaster? Why must I be the one to see the basket taken into the river and overturned by the tide? What was I to do then? Plunge in after it and risk drowning myself only to save a still-doomed child? Or what should I do if one of the Nile's infamous asps slithered into the basket, lured by the scent of warm, milky flesh? Must I wrestle the venomous snake away, letting its fangs close on my hand to protect my condemned brother?

The tears that had started for my mother and father and brother now fell hotly for myself, streaking my face, hot and dusty from the relentless sun. Thus absorbed with self-pity, I took no note of them until they were almost upon me. My breath caught in my throat as I choked on my sobs! Pharaoh's daughter! It could not be! Yet it was; she wore the ring of her father and her dress and bearing were that of Egyptian royalty. My heart beat like a trapped bird in my chest.

She had wandered some distance from the palace, and I could see her maids were annoyed, loath to follow her. There was no love between this princess and her women, that was clear from the dark looks they sent her when she was not watching. And she did not watch them; indeed, she barely attended them at all, and her disregard seemed deliberate. There was something in her face and demeanor that bespoke an anger still unknown to a child so young as myself. But I had an eerie sense of recognizing the roiling emotion I saw in her; I had just witnessed it in my brother, Aaron.

My curiosity fled when her eyes fell upon the basket. As if forgetting herself, she started toward it and then immediately halted and coldly directed one of her maids to retrieve it. The girl's eyes brimmed with curses, but she dared not utter them against Pharaoh's daughter. She reluctantly moved toward the basket, finally taking it up and bringing it to the princess, who snatched it rudely. I breathed out a silent gasp. Now my brother would die; for what else could be his fate at the hands of she whose own father had demanded the murder of all such infants? I closed my eyes, but could not stop the image of her flinging the babe into the river.

I could have had no image for what truly came next.

She barely glimpsed into the basket before slamming the lid closed. Her back to the maids, she was facing me, and I saw her eyes close tightly as she took one deep breath. When she opened her eyes, her face had become a marble mask as she told her maids haughtily, "Leave me. Now. Tarry at the bazaar if you will, I have no use for any of you." Torn between resentment at her tone and joy at the prospect of such freedom, they began moving away, hesitant at first, and then more rapidly as though afraid to risk losing such a boon. After assuring herself of solitude, she opened the basket and, a soft smile overspreading her hard features, gently touched my brother's face.

I watched in astonishment, confused as to what it meant. But when she lifted the babe, I suddenly feared she took such pleasure from the thought of hurling him into the river, and a soft cry escaped my lips. She whirled around, now clutching my brother to her, both fury and fear in her face. She saw me immediately and ordered me to come forth. Trembling, I did as bidden, but the sudden fear I'd seen in her eyes somehow made me brave. So when she demanded I explain myself, I instead asked her if she wished a nurse for the babe.

In my heart, I know now, I was still driven to please the mother who'd left me, and I spoke more for her than the infant. The princess studied me suspiciously, and then a dawning knowledge came over her face. Smiling grimly, she answered, "Bring her."

When my mother came, hope wild in her eyes and face, the princess told her to take and nurse the boy. Pharaoh's daughter warned us with dire threats that she would take the boy back when he was weaned, and though my mother's joy was dimmed, she had achieved her purpose against every odd. Within an hour the babe whom the princess called Moses, having taken him from the water, was back at my mother's breast in my father's house.

But everything had changed.

As if disturbed by the memory, I woke abruptly from my troubled dream and for a brief, blessed moment lingered in that soft place between slumber and consciousness of the many decades that had passed and the horror of leprosy. I fought waking, willing myself to return to sleep, even death, but I could not. Try as I might, I could not deny that the events of so many years ago had been the beginning of the travesty I now endured.

During the near three years Moses had remained with us, a precarious calm fell within our walls. But it was false for there was no true peace either in our family or our nation. The persecution of the Jews worsened, driven by Pharaoh's cruelty and fear; and as my father and brother were ground into exhaustion by relentlessly brutal labor, I was reminded again and again of the strange mixture of fear and rage in the face of Pharaoh's daughter. I came to understand how close in temperament was daughter to father.

Even as Egypt consumed the Hebrews, a more subtle force ate away at the fabric of our family. It was as if Moses, a child who grew more strange with each passing day, had brought a living unrest into our home. Even while growing healthy and strong, he seemed possessed of an extraordinary and endlessly watchful spirit. He never cried or misbehaved, but there was an unearthly quality about his gaze, which was continually fixed upon one of us. There was something in him that both attracted and frightened at once. Had the brief touch of Pharaoh's wild, restless daughter tainted him? Or was it our mother's obsessive devotion to him that so disturbed the tranquillity of our lives?

For obsessed she surely was. Just as Moses' attention was unwaveringly riveted on all around him, my mother's attention was riveted on him. That she favored him above all others and spoiled him terribly was indisputable. Yet it was more than that, something more disturbing and divisive. She believed she'd brought him back from the dead—and, I guess she had, in a way—and was determined that nothing would take him from her. Moses must have everything he wanted, and the strange babe had a way of communicating his desires to my mother without a cry or word.

When there was barely enough food for each of us to have a mouthful of supper, Moses had his fill. When the chill of the desert crept into our shabby home, the rest of us shivered in ragged robes while every blanket and covering was heaped upon the tiny child. While my father and Aaron suffered from strained muscles and sun-ravaged skin, what little ointment we had was slathered upon Moses. And when there was not enough water even to slake our thirsts, my mother gave Moses daily, cooling baths.

When my pitiable father remonstrated with her, softly so as not to shame her in front of us, "All cannot be lavished upon the boy. You have other children; what of them?" she'd snap defensively, "He is just a babe and cannot fend for himself, and you, his father, would steal the very food from his soft mouth!" Or a sly, ugly look would creep over her face and she'd answer, "I dare not deny the boy; would you have us risk the princess' wrath?"

Soon my father gave up entirely, his strong intelligent face becoming permanently etched with lines of sorrow and disappointment. He had little to do with Moses, and truly, my mother kept us all apart from her precious son as if we might harm him. And though I shiver to think on it now in my present dire state, my sisters and I murmured against the babe. Ignored by our mother in our simmering resentment, we did whisper of harming him. Oh, we spoke of merely pinching or teasing him, but the poison of envy flowed in us, and it was only our love—and perhaps pity?—for our father that stayed our mean, childish plans.

Denied the company of his wife and infant, my father, noting the growing ache in Aaron, became devoted to his eldest son. Laboring together by day, in the evenings my father taught Aaron the tenets and traditions of our people. He learned rapidly, and soon, father and son could be heard debating matters of faith—and the freedom my father hoped Yahweh would grant us—in the shadows of our diminished house. My mother, unaware of their very presence, hovered over the sleeping babe. Occasionally, Aaron's gaze would fall hopefully upon my mother, and the raw pain I saw in his eyes when she paid him no mind, pierced my young heart. I knew that all the attention my father paid Aaron could not atone for his mother's indifference.

My sisters and I yearned for the day Moses would be taken by the princess, but our hopes for a return to normal life were ill-founded. Though we dreamt of the days when the love between my father and mother illumined our home, those times were forever gone.

My mother suckled Moses long past the necessary time, and it was only when her breasts had no more milk, that she gave up. The princess, who'd insisted on meeting me regularly, demanded her "son." My mother, wild with grief, began to talk again about hiding the boy, but the princess weighted her queries with heavy threats. Our entire family would suffer her wrath if she was denied, and I made sure my father knew of this. For once he stood strong, insisting Moses be given to her. The wrenching and wailing that rent our home during those days beggar description, but in the end, my father prevailed and Moses was given over to his adoptive mother.

From that day forward, my own mother barely spoke to any of us.

Years later, when it was known that Moses had killed an Egyptian and then been betrayed by one of our own people and forced to flee the land, my mother blamed us. Her cold indifference turned to scorn. My sisters made poor marriages just to escape our dwelling, and Aaron, too, married early. I would never marry, I knew that well; I'd seen the result of marriage and the begetting of children. I wanted none of it. My brother, in the way we had between us, understood and made a place for me in his home. His wife and children accepted this; few dared challenge the bond that had grown stronger every year between Aaron and me. We did not see our mother, though our father was always welcome and frequently took his rest with us.

As time passed, there were rumors of Moses, that he had married a pagan—what else, given his upbringing; that he was known to have seen visions; and even that he walked with Yahweh. But for us, it seemed that the people spoke of a stranger. There was nothing to connect what we heard with the strange, headstrong child who'd caused such pain in the short time he lived with us.

Aaron was stunned when Moses summoned him. What could he want? How could this be? Our parents were both gone, and Moses was nothing but a discomfiting memory of which we never spoke. Aaron refused to

respond, but I was curious. And in the way I had with my brother, I per-
suaded him. In turn, Aaron would not go without me, and so, much to
the consternation of my sister-in-law, we agreed to meet Moses.

There was nothing of the arrogance we'd come to know and hear about
in the unkempt man who greeted us with an embrace. But while he'd lost
his hubris, Moses had grown even more disconcerting in his nature. It was
as if we faced a spirit who had somehow been clothed with human flesh
and blood. Even his embrace seemed to come from afar, and I could see
that he had to concentrate mightily in order to converse with us of simple matters. Soon he gave up altogether his attempt to make courteous
talk, and presented his plea with stark, shocking simplicity.

We were to help him free the Israelites from Pharaoh, who'd grown
even harder in his advanced age, and then lead them to some mystery
land that Yahweh had set aside.

I laughed aloud, and not kindly. But Aaron did not laugh. Aaron,
who at his father's knee, had learned the heritage and hope of our people, listened closely as Moses rattled on about visions of a burning bush
and Yahweh's instructions. Incredulous, I watched as this wild, bearded
stranger clothed in torn robes, convinced my beloved Aaron to join his
cause. I wanted to cry out and pull Aaron away; I wanted to fall upon
Moses and do him violence for disrupting our lives yet again; I wanted
to shout, "Don't you remember who this man is?!"

But I did none of these things, for I understood in those moments
that Aaron saw his own salvation. All that had been missing in his life
would be replaced by this man; Moses was offering him the chance to
both please the ghost of our implacable mother and fulfill the teachings
of our beloved father.

In the end I went along because I knew no other life than with Aaron.
And I suppose that in those early days through the plagues and
Pharaoh's deceptive promise of freedom, I thought to protect Aaron
from Moses' spell. But as the months and years passed, I was myself
drawn into the mystery of our younger brother. Inscrutable and remote,
there was something extraordinary about Moses. Basking in the shadow
of his power, I, too became a leader and prophetess of our people and
was accorded their respect. Was I not devout in my worship of Yahweh?

Had I not listened to all that my father taught Aaron? Did I not sing and dance about God's triumph over Pharaoh and his men in the Red Sea?

Still Moses and I never grew close; who could be close to the one who walked with God? Aaron was as near to our brother as any mere man could be, but it was the closeness of silence, not of comfort and fellowship. I was always the third one present, never equal and never quite comprehending the spirit and power of Moses. I did understand one thing: I had gone from being part of a beloved pair to being the one always looking on from the outside.

But whatever I felt about such rejection, whatever hollow bitterness echoed in me from the days of my mother, it could never excuse what I did. What brought me to this place of desiccation and shame.

The first crisis came as we struggled through the desert, searching for this elusive homeland that Yahweh had promised. Although, as I pointed out to Aaron as often as I dared, we only had Moses' word that Yahweh had even made such a vow. Would the God to Whom we all belonged speak only to one man? And one who had been raised a pagan and married so at that? Would the God of the Hebrews choose such a man—a half-Egyptian—over a man raised and schooled in the ways of our people? Aaron would not reply to my plaints, but as the people grew restive and our plight dire, he listened.

It was at this time, the most desperate in all the days and years we'd spent in the desert, that Moses was called to Mount Horeb by Yahweh to receive his law. Not understanding this mission, the people grew more discontented in their hunger and thirst and exhaustion. Without Moses to quell them, those few who were loudest and angriest cried out against Moses and even Yahweh. They grew violent in their protests, insisting that we had offended the pagan gods by fleeing Egypt and must make restitution. The few fomented riot, and the many, as always, followed.

Aaron was at first appalled, and then plainly frightened. When he turned his fearful, questioning gaze upon me, I saw the eyes of a boy who decades before had futilely sought comfort and approval from his mother.

Thinking no further, I said, "Tell the people to collect their gold and treasures."

We built a fire high and furious to forge the golden blasphemy. Many danced and sang and sinned around the creature in wild abandon as Aaron and I watched. Yahweh, who sees and knows all, sent Moses back to us, and it was to this sight that he returned. The humanity I saw then from my inhuman brother terrified me. Never, not even in my mother, had I seen such rage. Moses shattered the precious stone, and as he ground it under his feet, I understood that his humanity was not in his fury; it was simply in this: he had pled for us to Yahweh, and we had proved unworthy.

Yet even that was not enough to turn Moses—or God—against Aaron and me. Nor did I learn the lesson I was meant to from our betrayal of Moses at the foot of Horeb. My resentment remained as strong as my prophecies, and because I nurtured the former, the latter grew empty.

After Horeb, Moses grew even more distant. Continually in the presence of God, he had no need of human company, much less that of his brother and sister. His wife, the Cushite, took great pride in him and boasted day and night. And I, who had never loved nor married and would never hear the boasts of any husband, allowed my envy to be kindled. In turn, I sought to set the poison flowing in Aaron. "Are we not prophets of God?" I would hiss in his ear, "Have we not been the voice of God to the people when Moses was too mute to speak? Have we ever mingled our blood with a pagan spouse? Who is Moses, then, with his loud Cushite wife, to lord it over us?"

I shudder to think of the words I uttered, tempting Aaron until he joined my chorus. Moses easily ignored us, such was his nature. Yahweh did not. He summoned us to the tent of meeting with Moses. When I saw the mournful disappointment on Moses' face, my heart froze in terror: Aaron and I had provoked Yahweh beyond mercy. We entered the cloud from which God spoke to all but Moses—with whom he spoke directly—and the Lord breathed his terrible disapproval.

When he ceased speaking and the cloud departed, the leprosy was upon me.

Aaron groaned in agony, begging Moses to forgive me. But Moses, knowing forgiveness was not his to give in my case, beseeched Yahweh to have mercy upon me and make me clean. Yahweh, knowing my decades of hardness of heart, yielded to Moses but judged me still: I must remain a leper, outside the camp for seven days and seven nights.

Even as I opened my eyes from these wrenching memories, I saw the marks and sores that mirrored my diseased soul. The hours crept by, and with nothing to do but examine my heart, I felt true repentance for perhaps the first time in my life. As the sun and moon rose and set again and again, I watched our camp in the distance. I could hear our whole nation crying out to God for mercy upon their prophetess, and shame swept over me for the gifts I had squandered. Two figures kept a constant vigil, pacing the perimeters of our camp, their gaze fixed in my direction. Moses and Aaron. My brothers. I wept without end at the sight of them, and on the eighth morning I woke soaked in my own tears to find the leprosy gone and my skin restored.

Neither my brothers nor I ever set foot in the Promised Land, though our people did indeed enter according to Yahweh's word. Some say God dealt harshly with us, allowing us only a glimpse of this precious land. I don't think so. I've often thought it was as the one who came later, Jesus, said, "To whom much is given, much is expected." Each in our own way, I suppose we all three disappointed Yahweh. After all, he had given into our hands the fate and salvation of his chosen people, and we had not always done his bidding.

And quite apart from this, I am grateful that Yahweh showed us the Promised Land without bringing us inside its borders. Seeing over the centuries how the Israelites and other desert-dwelling nations have wasted, nay, devastated, the land that was Yahweh's gift, I am glad to have never traversed it. This way, I can hold to the dream of what it might have been. And hope for what it still may be. Because of all women, I know what is possible with God.

Active Meditation

We are, none of us, strangers to envy. And though, hopefully none of us will be rebuked by God as Miriam was, some of us may find our lives and achievements as poisoned by resentment as Miriam's extraordinary life and achievements were.

Envy is a powerful emotion. Has it crept into our lives? Are we jealous of a spouse's easy relationship with the children? Do we resent a sibling's favored position in the family? Do we seethe as a work colleague is lauded and promoted? Are we aggravated by the seeming unquestioning faith of someone at church? Do certain perpetually cheerful people drive us crazy because we can't seem to feel "up" all the time? Envy can easily sneak into a life, but it is not so easily expelled.

Remembering Miriam's seven days and seven nights of self-examination and repentance, let us honestly identify and confront our envy, and over the next seven days and nights, be aware of its negative impact on us. Each morning we can take time to form a strategy for banishing envy that day and each night review the effort. At the end of the seven days and seven nights, let us make a conscious effort to examine how our lives will be enriched by continuing to strive against envy.

Reflection/Discussion Questions

1. What was the role of Miriam's mother in shaping the adult she became?
2. Should her father have intervened, even if it meant risking his wife's wrath? Did he choose the lesser of two evils by at least keeping the home together?
3. How, if at all, has family-related envy impacted you and/or your family?
4. If you are a parent of more than one child, do you think you treat your children equally? Do you think your children would agree with your assessment?
5. Do you think people can truly change a negative habit like envy without a serious (or severe as in God's punishment of Miriam) impetus?

CHAPTER IV

Maala with Nao, Hegla, Mechla, and Thersa

Financial independence

NUMBERS, CHAPTERS 27, 36

Though forced to bear all the burdens and responsibilities of a man, I possessed none of the benefits. And yet, I needed the courage of ten men.

Because I was merely a woman my family was about to lose everything, even unto our very lives. Watching the grief-stricken faces of my four younger sisters, I knew I must act. But how? Where would I find the strength? Would I ever find the words? Would I even be granted an audience to make my plea? And, how would I begin to address the one known as "he who walks with Yahweh?"

I was only a woman.

Even more daunting, it was no simple request I must bring before Moses, the man of God. For Moses to even hear my plea, much less grant it, would require reversing centuries of law and tradition. It would mean that Moses—who had led us out of slavery, who had committed his life to preserving our heritage—would have to agree to change a tradition unbroken from the beginning of time: the law of male inheritance.

My heart pounded just thinking on it! How dare I bring such a request before such a man? What possible hope had I for success? What hope had I even to be granted a hearing? Despair threatened to overwhelm whatever weak resolve I might summon. I looked into the face of my youngest sister. Thersa had been our father's favorite, and she was devastated when he died during our nation's long meandering in the wilderness. Nor had she shown any signs of recovering since. Her eyes were still hollow with sorrow; how could she even begin to consider the implications of his death? Darkness smudged the sagging skin under her eyes; she looked so young, so lost, with no idea of our true plight.

And she was my responsibility.

They all were. I studied them each in turn. Nao, who'd been born just eleven months after me and had seemed bitter about it from her very first infant's wail. Hegla, the quiet one among us who'd clung to our mother and learned from her all the ways of making a home. Mechla, the rebellious one who sought always to win our mother's attention by making trouble, was utterly heartbroken when mother died in childbirth. Thersa, the babe born of that death, came late in my mother's life, ten years after Mechla, and might have been called a mistake in your world. But our father, far from resenting her, had loved her all the more for her resemblance to our mother. She was only eight years old.

He loved us all, in different ways perhaps, but we never doubted it. Indeed, his loving protection had turned out to be our greatest obstacle; none of us, not even I, Maala the eldest, had ever needed to fend for ourselves. He had taken care of everything, even as we wandered through the years in the desert. And now, at our journey's end, he was gone. As we sat, staring at each other months after burying him in a strange land, I knew that the burden fell upon me. But I was so ill-prepared! No daughter could inherit property—and our survival depended upon our receiving my father's portion in the new land. How dare I go before Moses to make such an unimaginable case?

As panic clamored in my head, an insidious sibilant voice whispered, "You know there is another way."

Groaning inwardly, I dropped my head in my hands. Yes, there was another way, but my heart cried out against it. It was what everyone expected of me, including my four watchful sisters. In fact, it seemed like the only solution. Except I abhorred it.

Zaccheus was a persistent man, of that I had no doubt. He had not hesitated to make his intentions plain to my father: he wished to marry me. From my father's perspective, the suit was not unwelcome. Though our father, Zelophehad of the Manassite clan, had undertaken the exile in the desert with some few possessions, he was not nearly as wealthy as Zaccheus. What small wealth my father had carried with him out of Egypt had been depleted in our wandering. And five daughters could be no more than a continuous drain unless they married well.

Zaccheus, by contrast, had wed in his youth, and his wife had died only after giving him four sons, all of whom strengthened their father's fortune. Had not Moses decreed, after the great census, that the Promised Land would be apportioned according to size of clan and number of sons? There had been no question of whether Zaccheus could provide well for me. For that matter, in my poor father's eyes, there had been no question of whether Zaccheus could provide for all of us, if need be, when we reached this Promised Land, a place that seemed more uncertain every day we languished in search of it. Besides his wealth, Zaccheus was a deeply respected and pious man of Israel.

He was also three decades my senior, bald with an unkempt grizzled beard, and he smelled suspiciously of the camels he'd kept in such generous numbers. Now I was no beauty, and as my father reminded me often and with little subtlety, time was passing. At the time of Zaccheus' suit, I was already twenty-four, well into, if not beyond, the acceptable age of marriage. Yet with all these factors working against me, I could not imagine myself with this ugly, old man. Some said as well that his wife had died of exhaustion, trying to satisfy his nature, which, it was whispered, was demanding…in every way.

My father frequently assured me that it would be a significant honor for me, at such a relatively young age, to become matron of a family that included four strong grown sons, their wives, and twenty-one children. But I'd heard all about this extensive family, and knew exactly what such an "honor" would entail. The wives bickered constantly, sometimes battling outright in the midst of the people over who deserved the greatest inheritance and whose son was most in favor. The vociferous envy between these contentious women was legend among Zaccheus' clan, and indeed, our entire clan and tribe. And their children? My stomach clenched just to think on what I'd heard about these twenty-one little plagues. Suffice it to say that they trod close in their mothers' footsteps, torturing each other and constantly causing mischief wherever we came to make camp.

Was this to be my solution? To marry the patriarch of such a monstrous family? I might have wished to follow my mother and father to a peaceful grave rather than face this. My father, to his everlasting credit, had been too kind when it came to it, to force me to wed Zaccheus. Indeed, Zelophehad of the Manassite clan was known in Israel as a gentle-hearted man, and his kindness did not fail within his own home as with some men. He understood my dread of Zaccheus and that troublesome tribe without my speaking a word, and though he sorely wished me to wed, he did not press it. Zaccheus' offer was courteously refused.

That was then. No sooner had my father died than Zaccheus resumed his suit. The lavish gifts and presumption that accompanied this renewal made my skin crawl. But why, after all, should he not presume? How else was I to save my family? How else were we to survive? How else was I to assure myself of a fair portion of the Promised Land, now that we were so very close at long last? My sisters and I had been born during this great wandering; we'd never known a true, steady home, and we hungered for the fulfillment of this promise. Our father had wanted it for us, and that we would be denied in life what he had lost in death was deeply galling.

Zaccheus knew all this. Who did not? Indeed, no Israelite expected me to do anything but accept Zaccheus; the foolish notion of bringing our case before Moses was unimaginable. Even I myself, despairing, had all but succumbed to Zaccheus' offer. Then, one morning, his eldest daughter-in-law called upon my sisters and me. And everything changed.

Harida was a singularly unpleasant woman. Grasping and avaricious, she was the chief troublemaker among the four wives of Zaccheus' sons; it was said that she was the one who time and again willfully rent what little peace might briefly fall among the four households. It became immediately evident that her intent in calling upon us was to bring pain and dismay.

She settled herself with great pomp and unconcealed disdain for our humble tent. Clearly, she disliked having to make this visit at all, which she did only at the unbreachable command of Zaccheus; and though he'd instructed her to make us feel welcome, such a thing was not possible for her. Instead, her natural animosity and greed compelled her to make it known that we would be an unwelcome addition, much resented by her and the other wives. Zaccheus' desire for a new wife—me!—was nothing but a thorn in her side, and she communicated this without hesitation.

Deliberately, Harida suggested that Moses would not settle as large a parcel of the Promised Land on Zaccheus as "some might assume." She looked pointedly at me as she said, "Ah, it's all up to Moses, isn't it? It is Moses who will apportion the land, and it may be that my poor father-in-law will not be as fortunate as others. Who can say but that we will end up scrabbling for our very lives? I cannot imagine how our poor father-in-law can even consider bringing a dower-less wife, not to mention her orphaned sisters, into such uncertainty! Of course, it is not as if any of you are accustomed to anything fine or of value."

She paused to look scornfully at our home and few shabby possessions before continuing relentlessly, "Of course, Moses should reward our beloved father-in-law for his piety and strong sons, but who can predict the whims of our great leader? After all what is Moses, really, but a strange, nearly mute man who claims to know Yahweh? What do we really know of him and his strange ways? Has he not elevated his haughty sister, Miriam, a mere woman, to the status of prophet, while all but ignoring his own sons? Has he not married a Cushite woman, forcing us to honor one we disdain?

"Ah, but who can say what such a man as he might do?"

Ah, but Harida, I mocked her silently as hope swept through me, who can predict what such a woman as I might do?

She had achieved her end, though not through the cruelty she intended. I waited in silent impatience for her to take her leave. When she finally did, my sisters, shamed and disheartened, were astonished at my demeanor. "What are you smirking about?" snapped Nao, "The woman has insulted us grievously and you are amused? Is that because you, at least, will have the status of wife, while we will grind out our lives under her foot?"

Accustomed to Nao's bitterness, I made no effort to dampen my excitement. Perhaps it was merely a fool's bravery, but Harida had formed my resolve. My mind returned again and again to the things she'd said about Moses, embracing her veiled condemnation of the man of God as though it had been praise. And truly, to my ears it had been just that. Moses was inscrutable! Who could say how he might judge or apportion the new land? Who could say how he might judge a person? Had he not, indeed, raised his sister, despite her envy and their long estrangement, far above the station of many men in our nation? Did he not, as Harida so sourly noted, love above any woman of Israel the Cushite who called him husband?

Would he not heed the word of God above the counsel of men?

Putting Harida and even Zaccheus out of my mind, I stunned my poor sisters further by ordering them, "Purify yourselves and dress in your best clothes. We have our own visit to pay." Nao opened her mouth to complain but the protest died on her lips when she looked at me. Not since our father's death had she seen me so determined, and I'd filled my voice with a confidence that brooked no argument. Regardless of what she might have wished, I was still the eldest.

My sisters were soon ready and gathered before me. From Thersa, who had felt my excitement and whose young eyes now shone with anticipation, to Hegla and Mechla who watched me curiously, to Nao who kept her sullen gaze averted, they stood waiting in silence. I cast my eyes over them as dispassionately as I could. Like mine, even their best clothes were aged by many washings, and we possessed no jewels or accoutrements to enliven our raiment. And yet, if I was correct in my hope, such a somber presentation would speak to our favor. Nao continued to glower, and I knew she was keeping silent with great difficulty, telling herself she would not give me the satisfaction of speaking again. I smiled inwardly and uttered the words that would shock even my second sister out of her bad humor.

"Come. We go before Moses in the Tent of Meeting."

My sisters gasped in unison, except for Thersa who eagerly gripped my outstretched hand as I strode out, not giving the rest a chance to protest. I heard Nao trailing behind and muttering to Mechla, but all three followed, not daring to be left behind. I understood their fear, but I could not abandon myself—or them—to it. Women did not enter the Tent of Meeting, much less present themselves to Moses. Such a thing was unknown in Israel.

And so, a hush descended over the assembly when we five entered. All prayer, all murmuring, yes even all motion, ceased. Every eye was upon us, but, breathing deeply, I kept my gaze upon only one. Thersa still grasping my hand, I moved forward slowly. I heard the soft rustle of my three sisters' robes as they followed, in my path. I knew my father's brothers were among the crowd, they who had offered us nothing upon my father's death, and I did not once turn my face to them. I did not dare, for such a sign of recognition would be enough for them to come forward and take me out, perhaps by force. I gave them no such opportunity. I knew well that the men of the Manassite clan would not willingly share their portion with their brother's orphan daughters. They, too, expected me to marry well and put an end to all speculation. And of course, there was Zaccheus near the front of the congregation, outrage writ large on his face. I nearly faltered, feeling their collective glare upon me, but at that moment there was a movement among those nearest Moses, and I saw Miriam watching me. Her expression, so often proud and cold, held a lively interest as she bent forward to speak in her brother's ear.

I took courage and continued on. It seemed we walked forever until I finally stood as close as I dared to Moses. He was seated in simple majesty, wearing a nomad's garb, and surrounded by his sister and counselors. I bowed low, but then straightened and raised my eyes to him, refusing to cringe like an unworthy supplicant. His gaze had remained upon the ground through all this, and with deepest trepidation, I watched his face for some sign. Excruciating moments passed before he slowly lifted his eyes to meet mine. He was an old, old man and more agonizing moments passed before he focused on our company. But when his eyes sharpened and studied me closely, I realized that his vision was not diminished by age; rather he was reluctant to exchange his contemplation of the Divine who was always with him for his duties to the people of God.

This revelation filled me with awe, and perhaps for the first time, I understood just what manner of man I now encountered. All words fled from my mind and tongue. My paralyzed silence stretched on, and Zaccheus started forward with authority. My throat closed in despair: now he would claim me, and all my hopes would come to naught. But then Moses raised his hand. It was a simple gesture, a mere movement, barely discernible. But Zaccheus saw it. The whole assembly saw it, and then watched him retreat in confusion. Standing behind Moses, Miriam smiled slightly, and I found my voice.

"My Lord Moses," I said and was immediately startled at the strength in my voice, "Our father has died in the wilderness and left us five daughters. Nor was he part of the rebellion in the company of Korah, but rather, he died in his own sin. Why should the name of our father be taken away from his clan because he had no son? Give to us a possession among our father's brothers."

I could hear discordant murmuring among my father's brothers, but after Moses' silencing of Zaccheus, none dared come forward to interfere with me. Moses observed me silently for some time, and then let his eyes rest on each of my sisters, ending with Thersa whereupon his face brightened for a moment. Finally he spoke, as much for the crowd as for us, "I will take this matter before the Lord, the God of Israel."

And as it turned out, the Lord, the God of Israel, did indeed approve that inheritance should pass to daughters. He decreed, through his servant Moses, that we were to have a portion in the new land, of our father's inheritance, among our father's brothers. And so it should be among all the tribes of Israel forever forward. My father's brothers of the clan of Manassite were furious and did prevail upon Moses to command that all daughters who inherit must marry into a clan of their father's tribe lest the inheritance pass out of the tribe. But this was of no matter to us, particularly as the Lord instructed Moses to add, "Let them marry whom they think best." There were many sons of my father's clan who were pleased to court women of property.

We, each of us, wed, though my own husband died within the year of our marriage leaving me without child. As the years passed, I took no other husband and having become the aunt to many, I wasted little time wishing for my own child. As to Zaccheus, he never married again, much to the delight of his avaricious sons and daughters-in-law. He lived long, and in the astonishing way of life, we came to be companions. With my own home and portion, I found it easy to ignore his pomp and arrogance, and he came to overlook what he called my "disproportionate" pride. At the end of his life, he would only allow me to tend him, ignoring the wails and gnashing teeth of his daughters-in-law and granddaughters and great-granddaughters. They would have been much more distraught had they known how many jewels and how much gold he urged upon me, begging me to take these gifts "lest those vultures get an even greater portion of my wealth."

The land Moses settled upon us was close to the border we crossed upon entering the Promised Land, and each year I undertook a solitary ritual. Traversing several miles, I came to the border and settled myself under one of the many cedar trees in that region, facing the mountain where Miriam had been buried. I went always on the anniversary of her death. I did not pray to her or speak her name. I merely rested, knowing that she had allowed me to enter into the place where she could not. And I was grateful.

Active Meditation

Like Maala, few of us examine our attitudes toward money and financial independence until circumstances force us to do so. However, this is an important exercise to undertake before it becomes necessary. Divide a page into three columns with these headings: Relationships, Expectations/Hopes, and Actions. Under Relationships, list the important relationships in your life, i.e., spouse, children, parents, employer. Under Expectations/Hopes, describe what you expect or hope for from that relationship regarding finances. For example, if you expect your parents to be financially independent as they age, state this clearly.

Now consider whether your true expectations are in keeping with the kind of person you wish to be. For example, if you honestly expect your spouse to handle all financial matters, ask yourself if such an expectation reflects your perception of yourself. Under Actions, list actions you can take to either change current patterns (i.e., if you perceive yourself as independent, you may want to work with your spouse on financial matters), or support your expectations (if you expect your folks to be financially secure as they age, you may want to begin communicating with them about their financial hopes and plans.

Be very honest as you complete this exercise; remember, you are the only one who will see it...and act on it.

Reflection/Discussion Questions

1. What role does money play in your personal and professional relationships?
2. Do you consider yourself financially independent?
3. What percentage of women who marry do you think expect to "be taken care of"?
4. Do you think most parents feel it is as important for their daughters to be financially independent as it is for their sons?
5. If you are (if not, imagine you are!) a parent, would you expect a son-in-law to be more financially capable than a daughter-in-law?

CHAPTER V

Deborah

Equality in judgment and battle

JUDGES, CHAPTERS 4—5

Women in your world have a saying: "A woman must work twice as hard to earn half as much as a man." This was true in my day, too, but my wages were the survival and piety of a nation, and the men I depended upon were weak and cowardly. Thank Yahweh for women warriors! For it was, indeed, a woman who saved Israel. Two, in fact.

I was a judge in Israel, a challenging enough job under the best of circumstances, but in my time, the nation had drifted far from our God, and my judgments, such as they were, had little impact on the people. My cry for a return to Yahweh and a rejection of idolatry too often went unheeded, and the wrath of Yahweh was kindled. In those days there was no king, and a judge such as I was considered the nation's leader. Yet my people did not heed the spirit of my judgment, though they never dared defy me on small matters. And what are small matters when a nation has no light or faith?

By the time I rose as judge before Israel, Moses had been long dead, and the people had conveniently forgotten the bravery of Joshua, whom God had ordained to drive out the enemies of Israel. No sooner had

Joshua died than did the Hebrews lose their heart, and soon after, their faith. Again and again, they turned from the worship of Yahweh to the worship of craven gods and idols, those useless images adored by other countries in the region. The mothers and fathers of Israel gave their daughters in marriage to sons of pagan clans, and they embraced pagan women as wives for their sons. And so, idolatry grew up in Israel, for surely these pagans would not come over to Yahweh when the Israelis themselves so quickly forsook their Lord.

Many times after the death of Joshua, our God raised up judges to cleanse Israel; and God would be with the judge of his choosing, and Israel would be cleansed. The people would repent at the word of the judge and turn back to God like children realizing how much they depend upon a parent. Yet at the death of each judge, as it had been at the death of Joshua, the people would lapse back into impiety and idolatry. What a hard-hearted people were my people!

In the days when I judged Israel, Yahweh had seemingly despaired of us. He had allowed foreign, pagan kings and their armies to overrun us. He made them our neighbors and allowed them to live amongst us. They grew strong, and our people grew weak and cowardly, afraid to challenge the might they saw all around them in the pagans. The Lord God finally gave us over into the hand of King Jabin, the Canaanite, who oppressed Israel for twenty years by the unconstrained hand of his general, Sisera. Sisera was infamous for his nine hundred chariots of iron and the cruelty with which he ruled his army and the nations he oppressed. The men of Israel withered at the very mention of his name.

The Hebrews piteously wailed that God had turned his face from us. As if we didn't richly deserve such a condemnation! But I knew, as prophetess and judge, that Yahweh would never truly turn his face from us. He merely waited in disappointment until we mustered the strength and faith to rise up against the enemies he had allowed into our midst and turn back to him. And so, I could do nothing but wait for God's word.

I was not idle. The Israelites streamed to me daily for judgment where I held my court, sitting under the what the people had come to call the palm of Deborah between Ramah and Bethel in the hill country of Ephraim. I judged between them, mediating both their petty and sub-

stantial disputes and dispensing judgment as the Lord God directed me.
For, indeed, the Lord did speak to me as he had to all legitimate judges
of Israel; as he had to Joshua, as he had to Moses, as he had to Abraham.

Do not mistake me: I make no boast here. To hear the word of God
is nothing to boast of; rather it is the most humbling experience one can
have. Moses, that great friend of Yahweh, knew this better than any man
or woman. Every judge, and I was no exception, learned this simple and
profound truth from Moses: one who hears the voice of God will never
again listen with great interest to any other voice.

How could we? Next to the sound of God, every other sound is mere
cacophony. Moses was known as a great prophet, yes, but also as a great
recluse. The closer he came to God, the farther he grew from those who
loved him in life. Such a thing is inevitable. Every judge experienced this
same unnerving phenomenon, though none of us achieved the intimacy with Yahweh that Moses had. But all of us suffered in our lives and
with our families. This was also inevitable.

I will not deny that I was lonely in my service of Yahweh, though I
would have never admitted it then. To have made such an acknowledg-
ment would have been to confess weakness, and that I could not do if I
was to lead my people. There were not a few among the high priests
who would have welcomed the opportunity to call me, a woman,
unworthy, and I had no intention of giving them such an opportunity.
But those of us called by Yahweh to judge Israel were set apart in an
indescribably complete way, as if a boundary was drawn over which we
could not cross into normal human intercourse, nor could others share
our sacred and terrible solitude. To be a woman chosen by God made
that boundary all the more distinct and unalterable. Male judges had, at
least, the love and respect of the other men who lead, the priests and
soldiers. But a female judge, though feared and revered for her status
with God, was still seen as something unnatural, a woman who would,
perforce, forsake wholly embracing the roles of wife and mother. The
men who judged Israel were heroes; I was an aberration.

My own beloved husband Lappidoth endured my silence and frequent absences with generous grace, but I can only imagine the cost to
him, the cost to us. I still do not like to think on it. No other call, no

other comfort, but the call and comfort of Yahweh could have been recompense. But with just such recompense, what else could truly matter?

And still, I never felt more puny or insignificant—more transformed and transparent—than in those moments when I breathlessly absorbed the words of Yahweh. It was only later, in the implementation of his will, that I became mighty.

He spoke to me in the twentieth year of the oppression of the Canaanite king and his general, Sisera. I spent a long, dark night, reclining under my palm, regaining the strength and energy that inevitably emptied from me whenever God's words filled me. By morning, I was ready to do his bidding. I sent for Barak, son of Abinoam, a good, if weak, man from Kedesh in Naphtali, and told him:

"The Lord, the God of Israel, commands you, Go, take position at Mount Tabor, bringing ten thousand from the tribe of Naphtali and the tribe of Zebulun. I will draw out Sisera, to meet you by the Wadi Kishon with his chariots and his troops; and I will give him into your hand."

As I had known he would be, Barak was immediately fearful. He did not wish to follow such a terrifying command, and thinking to thwart me, he replied, "If you will go with me, I will go. But if you will not go with me, I will not go." He smiled as he answered thus, believing a mere woman—who surely must be even more afraid than he—would never agree to go into such a perilous battle. But I was more than ready for this; after all, Yahweh had spoken, and what were the words of men next to his?

"I will surely go with you," I told him, barely able to keep the scorn from my voice. And I confess it was with some satisfaction that I added, "The road on which you are going will not lead to your glory, for the Lord will sell Sisera into the hand of a woman." Barak's face fell when he realized his lack of faith had not gone unnoticed. He glowered at me from below lowered eyebrows, thinking it was I to whom God would deliver the victory he coveted. Indeed, throughout the ages many have made this same error, assuming that because I certainly did go into battle against the Canaanites, that I was the woman chosen by God to vanquish Sisera.

Not true. I was God's judge; another woman was his warrior. Was the fact that she was not even a child of Israel a message from Yahweh to his chosen ones? Was it a warning that Israel must produce pious warriors worthy of God? Or was it a blessing, that he would deliver us even at the hands of a foreign woman? Who can say? I know only this: nothing from Yahweh is without intent.

Despite Sisera's ruthless nature and nine hundred chariots, despite Israel's poorly prepared and armed troops, the battle was easily won. Perhaps it was because of this quick miraculous victory, that people assumed I was God's victor. But Yahweh was triumphant at the Wadi Kishon because he used Sisera's iron chariots against him, sending a great rain that turned the valley to mud and all but immobilized the horses and chariots. Sisera's fearsome advantage became a fearful burden as the steeds screamed in frustration and the chariots sank. Sisera's army died there in the mud, under the sword of Israel. Only Sisera escaped.

Terrified for his life, he fled, not stopping until he was assured of safety. Or so he believed, for when he fled to the home of Heber, the Kenite, Sisera well knew that there was peace between Heber's clan and that of King Jabin. As commander of King Jabin's army, Sisera knew he would be welcome in the tent of Heber's wife Jael, and so he was. Heber and Jael lived near Kedesh; and when Sisera appeared, bedraggled, defeated, and afraid, Jael went out to meet him. Comforting him, she urged him to take shelter in her tent, offering him the finest milk when he humbly requested water.

Weary and vanquished, Sisera asked her to let no man come in to the tent while he slept. He begged her to deny that she had seen him or that she sheltered him should any man ask such things. Jael readily agreed, and she kept her promise. She told no man of Sisera's presence, nor did she allow any man to enter her tent where he slept. Instead she herself took up a tent peg, and creeping softly to where Sisera lay fast asleep, drove the peg through his temple until he was fast to the ground, dead.

Calmly she awaited the coming of Barak, who had pursued Sisera unto her very tent. She went out to meet Barak, who did not know what to expect, since Heber and Jael were known to have peaceful relations with the Canaanites. Jael greeted him quietly, saying only, "Come, and I will show you the man whom you are seeking." Silently, she led him into her tent where Sisera lay in a pool of weltering blood.

When Barak recounted this to me, I could see he was still aghast at the sight that had met him. And while pleased that such a victory had been granted Israel, he was frankly appalled that a woman had done this. For him, there was something as distasteful in this as there had been in my ready agreement to go to war. These were not the things that women did. We were unnatural.

Still, he joined me in the song of exultation that we sang before Israel and that was writ for all time in a sacred scroll. What choice did he have but to join me? Had not women delivered King Jabin and Sisera and the Canaanites directly into his hands? Had not women saved Israel? Had not Yahweh done as he'd promised and sold "Sisera into the hands of a woman?" So despite himself, Barak joined me in the song of triumph. We dressed in our finery and danced through the streets with the crowds of Israel whirling and rejoicing beside us as we praised Jael: "of tent-dwelling women most blessed."

And so she was, this tent-dwelling woman who had married into the clan descended from Hoab, the father-in-law of our beloved Moses. We had barely finished the song before I set about the business of securing the peace of my people so that I might be free to go to Jael. I wished to know this woman myself. Thinking on it now, I realize how I must have yearned to know a woman whose soul was like to my own; who was a warrior in the service of God just as I was a judge chosen by God. But at that time, I thought of none of these things; I simply wished to be away from Barak and the armies of Israel who resented giving credit to the women who had won the day. It seemed natural that I should go to Jael. It seemed necessary.

Just as she had gone out to greet and Sisera, just as she had walked out to meet Barak, so did she come out to meet me when I approached her tent at Elon-bezaanannim, near Kedesh. This was desert land, dry and arid, yet she had made a home of it and a flock grazed nearby. She greeted me simply and showed me the place in her tent where I might stay. I did not ask her whether it was the very place where Sisera had died at her hand. There was a peace about her which I found unassailable, but also reassuring as, I imagined, had Sisera. She seldom spoke, and yet I found myself comforted by her very presence, so much so that

I ended up staying with her much longer than I'd intended, through the four phases of one entire moon.

I had gone to her, wanting to ask why she had killed Sisera. Why had she risked the peace between the clan of Heber and King Jabin? Why had she courted the wrath of the Canaanites? Was her husband, Heber, aware of what she'd planned? Had he approved? Or had she not even asked him? Had she acted in reverence for Hoab, and through him, Moses? Or had Yahweh come to her directly, as he came to me, and told her to vanquish the enemy of Israel?

But when she met me, the questions died in my heart. I knew she would not answer. I knew without asking. She was not a woman who felt the need to speak or to explain herself, even to the judge of Israel. If I'd had a notion to play the sovereign with her, it dissipated before she'd even finished her brief greeting. No one would govern this tent-dwelling woman, and I felt a flooding sense of relief as that revelation swept through me. With her, I could be myself, Deborah. Not the judge. Not the wife. Not the goader of men, without whom they would languish in cowardice. Not the person upon whom a nation depended. With Jael, I was another descendant of tent-dwellers, and I was grateful for the respite she offered me as companion and equal.

I'd brought her a treasure in jewels as a gift of thanks from the people of Israel. When I spilled them out before her in their glorious, shimmering, luminescent hues and made my explanation, she gave a small smile. Then she rewrapped them in their soft, polishing cloth and placed them in a basket near where she slept. I doubt she ever wore them, and in retrospect, having come to know her, I could probably have not offered a less suitable gift to this woman. I like to think she at least looked at them upon occasion and took delight in their beauty.

The days passed more quickly than any before or since. We did nothing of import. I soon learned her routine, the many tasks she must undertake each day to keep herself and her clan alive and flourishing. Her work was hard, her life might have seemed tedious, but I reveled in the simple chores that brought, at first, aching muscles, and later, strength. After a month with her, spent mostly tending her small herd of goats, I understood how she could have lifted the workman's mallet and driven the peg through Sisera's skull. We seldom spoke, understanding one another without words, and after years of people bringing their plaints and pleas to me, I found the silence sweet.

I knew I could not stay with her forever. My people were a childish, inattentive people; in my absence they would soon grow restive. It was past time to resume my place under the palm of Deborah, and when I left Jael, our parting was as unremarkable and gentle as our meeting had been. No tears were shed, or promises made, as sometimes are between friends who must be separated. Rather I went on my way, sorrowing but renewed, and the one time I ventured to glance back at her, Jael had already returned to the goats, her back to me.

I ruled Israel in peace for forty years after the death of Sisera and the triumph over Jabin. No other tribe or clan or people dared disturb us during these years for the word had gone out: Israel was ruled by a woman of great might and power to whom God listened. If the God of Israel could destroy Jabin at the hands of a woman, than who could prevail against his people?

Ah, I would think to myself as my reputation grew and spread, but it was at the hands of two women, was it not? Was God not with Jael as powerfully as he was with me?

As the years passed, I thought of her frequently. We never spent another moment together, or exchanged missives as we might easily have. What words would we use? What was there to say?

Upon occasion, I would take an hour or two and seclude myself from the hordes of Israel. In those precious moments, I would settle myself with the sacred scroll in which was recorded the song of exultation we sang after the victory over the Canaanites. I would read again and again the words that praised Jael, and even those that told of my awakening to the call of God. Sometimes I would grow somber as I saw the words and considered what they signified, what price was paid for the sanctity and freedom of Israel.

But then I would think of the women who had paid such a price for our people before Jael, before me. Sarai, who put aside her tenderness to become a formidable leader first and a wife second. Rebekah, who used deceit and risked the love of her clan and husband to put forward the son who must anchor our people. Miriam, who cared not for the opinion of any man, and who sang and danced in exultation at the destruction of Pharaoh's men in the Red Sea.

In these sacred, silent times, I would think of these, our women. I would think of Jael. I would think of myself. I would think of those to come. And I was content.

Active Meditation

Women today who lead in their professions and in government or serve in the military have it as difficult as Deborah. Indeed, they probably have it more difficult because they can't claim that God ordained them to serve in these positions! Still, the number of women in positions of power or leadership is steadily, if slowly, increasing. You probably know such a woman. Perhaps she is a friend, family member, or colleague. Or maybe she is someone you've heard or read about: a judge who made a courageous decision; a policewoman or soldier; a politician; a doctor; a renowned teacher.

Whether you know her personally, or just through her reputation, take the time to write to her. Tell her that you admire her and appreciate the sacrifices she has made for her work and her position. Let her know that you consider her an inspiration, and that you will pray for her. Then do it.

Reflection/Discussion Questions

1. Do you believe that "a woman must work twice as hard to earn half as much" as a man?
2. Do you think women are still expected to be wives and mothers, regardless of what other objectives they establish and achieve?
3. If you are a single working woman, how do you feel people generally perceive your lifestyle and choices?
4. If you are married with children and work outside your home, how do you feel you are perceived? If you work at home raising your family, how do you feel you are perceived?
5. Does your church offer appropriate and equal roles for women?

CHAPTER VI

Ruth

Loyalty

RUTH, CHAPTERS 1—4

When my young husband died not long after his only brother, everyone told me the same thing: Go home. Return to the home of your mother and father. Start again. Seek another husband who will not die before he gives you children to fill your womb. Even my beloved mother-in-law, Naomi, though she was now utterly alone and without recourse, her husband having died years before her sons, said the same.

The truth is I did not want to go home.

I had been with my poor husband, Mahlon, for almost a decade, and his family had become my family. His father, Elimelech, had treated me with more respect and kindness than I ever received at the hands of my own father; and his mother, Naomi, had taken me to her heart in a way I'd never known in my own home from my own mother. The idea of abandoning Naomi, of returning to the household and parents who had been only too happy to sell me to an unfamiliar Israelite husband when I was barely more than a child, made me ill.

And more important by my way of thinking, there was Yahweh. Having come to know the power and the majesty of the God of the

Hebrews, I could not possibly return to the worship of the people of Moab, for such were my parents and ancestors. Could I ever again bring myself to adore pagan idols after knowing the glory and faithfulness of Yahweh? Could I resume praying to petty, useless gods after years of bringing my petitions to the one, true God? Could I go back to the baseless superstitions of my family after witnessing the trusting faith of Naomi and Elimelech?

No. I would not go back. I could not.

Yet everyone seemed determined to convince me I must. After all, my own people argued, Naomi and Elimelech were Jews of Ephrathah, strangers in our land. They had fled to Moab with their sons, Mahlon and Chilion, from Bethlehem in Judah years before when a brutal famine struck their own land. Naomi and Elimelech came here to survive the famine, and once established, took for their sons myself and another Moabitess named Orpah as wives. Elimelech had died shortly after our weddings, and then a decade later, Naomi also lost both her sons.

But that was not my problem, the Moabites assured me. I was now free to stay in my country, to embrace our ways and religion, to resume the life I'd known as a child. And I was free to marry again, my own parents urged me, their eyes gleaming at the thought of a second dowry. "This time I will find a husband of Moab," my father declared as though he'd made a mistake in my first husband, "He will be man enough to give you sons and me grandsons. A man of our world and culture." Yes, I thought silently, a man from Moab who will add to your store of wealth, the very riches you were pleased to increase by extorting a ridiculous bride price from Elimelech and Naomi when they chose me for Mahlon.

I heeded not my parents or my people. There was only one opinion I cared about, but alas, even that one appeared set against me. Naomi joined the chorus of those demanding that my sister-in-law Orpah and I stay in Moab and return to our families. Naomi herself was about to return to Bethlehem, having received word from her kin that the famine had ended; and despite the great love that had grown up between us, she was filled with the hopeless grief of a widow who'd also watched her only sons die. So she told us, "Go back each of you to your mother's house. May the Lord deal kindly with you, as you have dealt with the dead and with me. The Lord grant that you may find security, each of you in the house of your husband."

When both Orpah and I insisted on returning with her to Bethlehem, her weary despair spoke out against our pledge, "Why will you go with me? Do I still have sons in my womb that they may become your husbands? Turn back, my daughters, for I am too old to have a husband. Even if I thought there was hope for me, even if I should have a husband tonight and bear sons, would you then wait until they were grown?"

In fact, Naomi was still young enough to marry, but I knew she never would; her sorrow was too heavy, and that alone resolved me to stay with her. I was all she had, and I knew she would never have sons unless I someday gave her one. But her words either frightened or convinced Orpah, for she kissed us tearfully and turned back to her family in Moab. However, I would not leave Naomi's side, and I pleaded with her, "Do not press me to leave you! Where you go, I will go; where you lodge, I will lodge; your people shall be my people, and your God my God. Where you die, I will die—there will I be buried. May the Lord do thus and so to me and more as well, if even death parts me from you!"

Naomi embraced me silently. There were no more words of our parting. We made the arduous journey to her former home in Bethlehem, arriving at the beginning of the barley and grain harvest. Although the Jews there at first rejoiced upon seeing Naomi, they soon mourned with her for the loss of Elimelech, Mahlon and Chilion. And though her people welcomed her, we still had to find means to support ourselves; there were no husbands or sons to provide for us. I received her permission to go into the fields and follow after the reapers, gleaning what I could of the ears of grain. I hoped in my heart to find favor with whomever owned the fields, that he might hire me to work with his other young women as a reaper; but even if I was not hired, at least I might collect enough grain to keep us fed.

The Lord God blessed me on the very first day, for when I followed behind the gleaners, they did not deter me. I had collected a good amount of grain through all the morning hours when Boaz, the field's owner, came to see how his harvest progressed. Though I did not know him by sight, I knew he was kin to Elimelech because Naomi had spoken well of him. Nevertheless, my heart was filled with dread when he called me forth after conferring with his reapers. After all, I was a foreigner in his land, the former pagan wife of one of his kin. What right had I here? Trembling, I came forward.

I had nothing to fear. Boaz spoke kindly to me, urging me to remain in his field and follow after his young women, gleaning all I might want. He gave orders that no man was to interfere with me. I was overcome with this blessing Yahweh had granted me, and I fell at Boaz's feet in humble gratitude. Wishing to ease my discomfort, he raised me up and gave me to know that he had heard of my loyalty to Naomi and wished to favor me for it. "May you have a full reward from the Lord, the God of Israel, under whose wings you have come for refuge!" he proclaimed, and then urged me to join his young women in their daily meal. I had not eaten so well since leaving Moab, and yet no one looked askance at me for my hearty appetite. Indeed, Boaz instructed his people to feed me well and to make sure I left that day with ample grain.

Naomi was very pleased when I returned home, laden with grain and full of news about Boaz. She assured me that he was nearly "next of kin," the one with the right to redeem, and the one who might be our help in these difficult times. I knew my mother-in-law well; it continued to goad her that I should be with no husband at such a young age. I knew she still blamed herself in that she had allowed me to come with her, and so I was troubled but not surprised when she revealed her plan to attach me to Boaz. Her instructions were simple: I was to wash and anoint myself, dressing as well as my poor store of clothing would allow; conceal myself on his threshing floor until he'd eaten and imbibed liberally; and once he slept, uncover his feet and lie down there.

I was more than a little dismayed at her words. Embarrassment and uncertainty flooded through me, mixed I must admit, with a certain sort of excitement. Though so much older and not so handsome as Mahlon, Boaz had stirred something in me—something I thought had died with my husband. Still I was uncomfortable taking such bold action, and in the end I obeyed Naomi simply because I loved her. I knew she wanted what was best for me, and in her land, I would do as I promised and embrace her ways.

My heart beating wildly, I watched and waited from my concealed place until Boaz ate and drank his fill and went to sleep. Then I crept from my place and laid at his feet, remaining motionless, hardly daring to breathe and certainly not able to sleep. After what seemed to be the passing of many seasons, though it was probably just after midnight, Boaz awoke. Astonished to see me there and unable to immediately recognize me in the pitch night, he asked who I was. When I told him, using the words Naomi had given me, he was all the more amazed. Still, he revealed the depth of his generous and decent nature, telling me, "May you be blessed by the Lord, my daughter, this last instance of your loyalty is better than the first; you have not gone after young men."

But Boaz then told me there was a problem. Though he was a near kinsman, and Naomi had obviously selected him deliberately, there was one other kinsman who was closer. This man, then, came before Boaz in having the right to redeem, or as you might say in your world, the "right of first refusal"!

Though Boaz spoke kindly, I was devastated! Who might this stranger be, this one who could claim me so easily? And why had I allowed myself to humble myself before Boaz if another had the right to me? Why had Naomi allowed this to happen?

Boaz must have seen my distress for he hastened to reassure me that all would be well. If this man, this next of kin, did not choose to have me—for that is really what we were talking about, in plain words—then Boaz himself would do so. I could not bring myself to tell him what small consolation this was! I knew he meant well, but I dreaded the thought of marrying another. I could not yet admit that what I felt for Boaz was love, but I surely knew that I couldn't bear being wed to some stranger like so much chattel.

After letting me rest there for the night, he sent me off before dawn, lest I be seen and my reputation ruined. Before I left, he again tried to comfort me and filled my apron with grain, urging me to bring the bounty to Naomi. I returned to my mother-in-law with a heavy heart, and it was only at her words that I realized I might have underestimated Boaz. She certainly had not, and she told me so, "Wait until you learn how the matter turns out, for the man will not rest, but will settle the matter today."

Though I saw no reason for her optimism, I tried to take heart. It was the longest day of my life, even longer than the day my poor Mahlon had died. By evening, the word began spreading through Bethlehem like a locust swarm: the great man and landowner, Boaz, was to take a wife! And it would be Ruth, the Moabitess, the widow of his kinsman Mahlon!

Me. It was to be me! Boaz had somehow won me from the man who was Elimelech's next of kin. My heart rejoiced in a way, I am still reluctant to admit, it had not when I'd learned I was to wed Mahlon a decade earlier. Then I knew nothing of my future husband, only that some Jews who'd fled the famine in Bethlehem had the money to purchase a Moabite bride for their son. And though I grew to love Mahlon, I knew nothing of him at first, and I was just a child then. Boaz, I already knew, and I had experienced his goodness. And I was no longer a frightened child; I could well imagine the pleasures as well as the security that would come with marriage to such a man.

Later that night I learned how Boaz had won me. I had known he was decent and kind, I now learned that he was clever as well. No sooner had he left me at the dawn, than he had gone up to the gate of the city. He waited there until the man who was next of kin passed. Boaz called him, and, in the way of the Hebrew people, also summoned ten of the elders of the city. When they had gathered Boaz told the next of kin, in the hearing of all present, that Naomi was selling a parcel of land. Since this land belonged to Elimelech, Boaz continued, it was the right of the next of kin to buy, or redeem, the parcel of land.

Boaz let the man know, in front of the ten elders and all the city, that since he was the next of kin, he had the right to buy the parcel. But, Boaz added, if the man would not redeem the property, then Boaz himself was next in line of kin and would redeem it himself.

The man who was next of kin promptly committed himself to buying the parcel. When I heard this, I was grateful that I had not been witness to this council, for I would have despaired at this commitment, believing the inevitable: that I would have to marry him. But Boaz, my clever husband-to-be, was not finished. After the man affirmed his willingness to buy the property, Boaz added an important condition, telling the man and all those who were present, "The day you acquire the land, you are also acquiring Ruth, the Moabite, the widow of the dead man, to maintain the dead man's name on his inheritance."

Boaz well knew what the man's reaction would be to such a condition for the man had his own inheritance to maintain and would not risk it by bringing another man's name into his family. As Boaz had known he would, the next of kin immediately relinquished his claim, acknowledging that he could not damage his own inheritance in such a manner. Then Boaz, having his achieved his end with great subtlety and skill, proclaimed before all assembled that he would acquire the property and with it, Ruth, as his wife. In so doing, he pledged, he would maintain the dead man's name on his inheritance so that Mahlon's name would not die out from his people. What he left unsaid, but what was understood by all the people, was that Boaz would also care for Naomi, keeping her as her sons would have. To mark the contract, the next of kin removed his sandal and gave it to Boaz, and thus, the contract was made.

When the people of Bethlehem told me of Boaz's manner and wisdom before all assembled in this matter, my secret delight in the thought of becoming his wife was deepened by my pride in his power and intellect. Mahlon had been a sweet, gentle man, as naive and young as I had been. We emerged from childhood to adulthood together and our love grew with us. But what I felt for this man, who was older and more experienced than I, was something different, something I could not really put into words. I know only that I was lit with a slow flame from within, and I looked forward to our marriage with hope and desire unlike anything I'd felt in the whole of my life.

Our wedding was as festive an affair as it could be, given my widowhood. Boaz's public commitment to keeping Mahlon's name in the inheritance of his people allowed for much more rejoicing than might otherwise have been possible. The people understood that our marriage was, indeed, a redemption of Mahlon and even Elimelech and Naomi, rather than an rejection of the past. Boaz was a wealthy man, and our wedding was the occasion of much celebrating and feasting among all the people of our village. Even those who had gleaned with me in the fields during those early days were given places of honor. And during all of this I observed my new husband with a warm regard and pleasure.

Accordingly, it was not long after we were married that the Lord, the God of Israel further favored us, giving us a son. My pleasure in my son, whom we named Obed, was the quiet delight of a mother, but the ecstasy of Boaz and Naomi knew no bounds. I cannot say, even now, who was more overcome with joy—my son's father, or his grandmother! The women of Bethlehem rejoiced wildly with Naomi, singing, "Blessed be the Lord, who has not left you this day without next of kin; and may his name be renowned in Israel! He shall be to you a restorer of life and a nourisher of your old age; for your daughter-in-law who loves you, who is more to you than seven sons, has borne him."

My honored mother-in-law virtually glowed with happiness, and she took Obed to herself, becoming his nurse. Boaz, ever kind and discerning, accepted this with great equanimity, knowing the boy would be cherished and raised in the way of his ancestors and according to the precepts of Yahweh. And so Naomi and Boaz raised our son according to the traditions of Israel and in the shadow of the Lord's protection. Obed grew in strength and spirit, an honor to his father and grandmother, beloved by me, and pleasing in the sight of the Lord. It was only as the generations passed that we came to understand just how important a role our son would play in the redemption of Israel.

Obed came of age, married, and had his own sons, among them Jesse, my handsome and fruitful grandson who, in his own turn, had a number of lusty, strapping sons. The last and seemingly least likely of them, David, became he who would be the first great King of Israel. It has always seemed a lovely irony to me that David, the great-grandson of the widowed Moabitess and like her, the "outsider" among his brothers, was the one selected by Yahweh to lead Israel into a new age of greatness. And it was to be recorded that from David's line would come another king, Jesus, he who would change the world.

Through the ages, some have said that all this came about through my loyalty to Naomi, and surely I did love my mother-in-law and attach myself to her in the way of a devoted daughter. Yet I know it was Yahweh who set me on the path to Bethlehem, for I was as unwilling to leave him as I was to abandon Naomi.

And I take little pride in the world's perception of my loyalty. It is not that I am so humble, though I strive to be, but that I've come to believe that loyalty is a complex thing. Is it not true that in pledging loyalty to one, a person must be somehow disloyal to another? In my loyalty to Naomi and the inheritance of Mahlon, was I not disloyal to my parents and the inheritance they wished to preserve? Was my dedication to Yahweh and Naomi a true selfless act, or was it a refusal to return to a life that had lost all appeal?

I think of our women and wonder how loyalty has defined their actions and our history. Has it always rewarded them as it surely rewarded me? Has it always benefited those they love as it surely benefited those I loved? In Miriam's loyalty to Aaron, was she not, at least for a time, disloyal to Moses? In Rebekah's loyalty to one son, Jacob, did she not betray the other, Esau? In Leah's loyalty to her father, did she not deceive Jacob, her husband? In Deborah's loyalty to Israel, did she not neglect her own husband and family?

And much later, did not the Magdalene pledge herself and alter her entire life in loyalty to the one who was to come, only to have abuse and scorn heaped upon her?

Can anyone say what loyalty has meant to our women through the ages? Can anyone name its cost? Is it always a virtue? Was it with me?

Active Meditation

Ruth has become, through the centuries, the embodiment of loyalty. And though Ruth was handsomely rewarded, the decision to be loyal to God or to a person or to an ideal does not always bring obvious rewards. For example, remaining loyal in a marriage where the other partner is not can be an agonizing experience. And in some cases, loyalty can become a crutch, something that allows us to avoid hearing God's message or making a healthy change.

Examine your life for instances when you've exhibited loyalty that could be considered—like Ruth's—above and beyond the call of duty. Select two specific cases: one in which you honestly believe your loyalty was based on a well-founded, faith-filled decision; and the other which, in the clear light of twenty-twenty hindsight, you feel your loyalty may have been ill-considered or based on the wrong reasons. What makes these two instances different? Were you as sure in your commitment in the second case as you were in the first? Did you have doubts? Did you follow your true instinct in both cases? What role did God and prayer play in both decisions?

Use the answers to these questions when you consider pledging loyalty in future instances.

Reflection/Discussion Questions

1. Are there instances when loyalty is always "right" regardless of the cost, i.e., in a marriage, toward parents, etc.?
2. Have you ever been in a situation where loyalty to one has required a form of disloyalty to another?
3. Do you feel greater loyalty to God than to your church, or do you feel they are one and the same? How do you define loyalty in terms of religion?
4. What is the greatest price you've paid for your loyalty?
5. What is the greatest reward you've experienced for your loyalty?

CHAPTER VII

Hannah

Relentless prayer

I SAMUEL, CHAPTERS 1—4

Every newborn infant was a dagger plunged into my heart.

Every babe consecrated to Yahweh with the proper gifts and rituals tore my spirit in two. Every toddler, clinging to his mother's skirt and peeking out with large, dark eyes, rent me asunder. Every thirteen-year-old boy brought to read and pray in the temple for the first time as a man wrenched my innards with unendurable pain. Every son who took a wife in the prescribed festival before his family and village sent fire through my mind, blinding me to all but what I lacked.

And every woman, heavy with child, was a reproach to my eyes and ears and soul.

Such was my disgrace and agony before God and men. I hid it well. None, looking upon me in those moments, would have glimpsed my anguished yearning. None would have discerned the wounds that had come to abide in me like leprosy that would not be cured. Yet they must have guessed. For even as I smiled and nodded and attended every event and ceremony, even as I rocked every infant in my arms, bounced every small child on my knee, praised God for every passage into manhood, and rejoiced with every mother who saw her son wed, they must have pitied me in their hearts. They must have spoken of me at the well and in their homes and in all the places where my absence surely loosened their tongues.

"Poor Hannah," they must have said, "No child yet, and at her age!"

"What has Hannah done to so offend the Lord, the God of Israel, that he has closed her womb?"

"What sin keeps Hannah's marriage childless?"

"What sorrow must fill her house and poison the heart of Elkanah, her husband!"

"How fortunate for Elkanah that he has Peninnah to give him abundant children. God has certainly not closed her womb!"

For me, this was the final, deepest cut. My husband Elkanah had married another wife, Peninnah, who had given him many children almost from the first time he lay with her, she frequently claimed to any who would listen. And though he loved me utterly, and gave me double her portion at the yearly time of sacrifice, even his love could not take away my shame and longing for a child. It was with me and Peninnah as it had been with Sarah and Hagar, and as with Rachel and Leah. Just as Sarah knew how Abraham loved her above all others, and just as Rachel knew how Jacob loved her above all others, I knew that Elkanah loved me above all others. But as with Sarah and Rachel, it mattered little as long as I had no son.

Recognizing my grief as one who shares the same household must, Peninnah rubbed salt into my wounds at every opportunity. Her envy of Elkanah's love for me made her vicious and unrelenting in her provocation. She often demanded my help with her brood, knowing how deeply it pained me to see the bearing and resemblance of my husband in her beautiful children. Claiming that she was too exhausted to care for them herself, she would sigh, "You can surely help me! What else do you, childless as you are, have to do? Besides, I am weary. It is too much for one woman to bear Elkanah's attentions and the babes born of them! It seems I need only lie with him once to be with child again."

Or, she would taunt, as she held her latest babe aloft for all to admire, "How fortunate for Elkanah that I am so fruitful. At least no one will think that he is not man enough to give a real woman children. At least all will know where the fault is. He need not feel ashamed!"

And this truth made my humiliation complete. Though I am ashamed to admit it, I would have preferred it if my husband had been childless, for then no one could have placed the blame so surely upon me. That he had children by Peninnah—and children in abundance—proved not only that he was fertile, but that I was barren. The evidence was everywhere as Peninnah's children were well-known in our village, Ramah, and were allowed to roam freely among the people. I think Peninnah gloried in shaming me by keeping her children in the sight of all.

The worst of it came during the yearly sacrifice. At this time each year Elkanah was in the habit of leaving Ramah in Ephraim to worship and sacrifice to the Lord at Shiloh where the priest Eli and sons presided. Each year we would go up, and each year Elkanah, on the day of his sacrifice, would give a portion to Peninnah and each of her children. To me, he would give a double portion to signify his love for me and how well he understood my suffering. But this gift in itself became a chastisement when Peninnah, jealous of our husband's love and generosity, would mock me, hissing, "He gives you more out of pity, not love. He gives to you out of guilt as he would give to an addled relation of whom he was ashamed."

I endured her stinging words year after year, half-convinced myself that she was right. Far from reproaching me, Elkanah, who never witnessed her attacks because she was careful, ceaselessly sought to comfort me. "Hannah, why do you weep?" he would ask, his face full of concern, "Why do you not eat? Why is your heart sad? Am I not more to you than ten sons?" He never cared about my barren womb; still this constant love made me desire all the more to bear him a son. Even his tender solace became a knife twisting in my gut.

Finally a year came when, after journeying to Shiloh, I was driven half-mad with my own sorrow and Peninnah's cruelty. After the ritual sacrifice, I rose up from the table, and presented myself alone in the temple at Shiloh before the Lord, the God of Hosts. For years I had prayed him to give me a son, but this was different. I was beyond hope. I had nothing to offer the Lord, all my substance was poured out in spent longing and surrender. I could do little but weep, and unable to do anything of or for myself, I prayed, "O Lord of hosts, if only you will look on the misery of your servant, and remember me, and not forget your servant, but will give to your servant a male child, then I will set him before you as a one consecrated and given to you until the day of his death."

In all the years of my resentment and bitterness, I had never prayed in such a way. I had never offered to give back to God what I begged him to give to me. Yet this prayer, made from the depths of my misery and despair, emerged from the true essence of my soul. There was nothing in it of selfishness; I merely joined myself for the first time to the will of the Lord.

In my distress and revelation, I was unaware of Eli, the priest, as he stood and watched my lips move in fervent prayer. I must have seemed mad to him for he rebuked me, thinking I was drunk and making a mockery of prayer. When I told him of my deep distress and the raw sincerity of my prayer, though I did not reveal the content, he reassured me, "The God of Israel will grant the petition you have made to him." At peace for the first time since my marriage, I rose from my knees and returned to my husband. Peninnah, for all her efforts during our return journey to Ramah, could not touch me with her words.

No sooner had I arrived home and lain with my husband than did I conceive. The Lord had heard the pouring out of my soul. He gave me a son, whom I named Samuel, to signify for all that I had asked the Lord for him. Elkanah was beside himself with joy, though I can say even in this, my kind husband was true: he rejoiced for my happiness and fulfillment more than for himself; his steadfast love for me remained unaltered even by the birth of our son. And it was a good thing, too, for I fully intended to fulfill the offer I had made to the Lord with my whole being.

Peninnah was also beside herself, but not with joy. The conception and birth of Samuel diminished her, removing her power over me and reducing her status in the eyes of our village. Elkanah did not treat her any less kindly, but he had never made a secret of his surpassing love for me; and now the whole of our people knew that the barren wife whom he'd loved for so long—seemingly without reason—had borne a child. And not just any child, but a nazirite, a consecrated boy to be dedicated to God. People rejoiced doubly for this miracle, and all those who'd murmured about my womb being closed as a punishment now proclaimed that my womb had been opened as a sign of extreme favor.

Peninnah could do little more than mutter and gnash her teeth, as Samuel became the beloved child of Ramah. She even refused to let her children play with their little brother, and this suited me well, for I knew I'd have but a little time with my son and was happy to keep him to myself.

Elkanah, in keeping with his gentle, affable nature, made no protest when I told him of my promise to God and my intention to keep it. Fearing that he would be angry or miscomprehend, I'd dreaded telling him and waited until the time of year came for us to journey to Shiloh for the sacrifice. Vanquishing my fear by force of my will, I came to my husband during the time of preparation for the pilgrimage and said, "I will not go up to this sacrifice. As soon as the child is weaned, I will bring him, that he may appear in the presence of the Lord, and remain there forever; I will offer him as a nazirite for all time."

He demanded no more explanation and told me to do as seemed best to me. And so, I nursed my son, lavishing all my time and attention on him, knowing that I would soon give him to God. It was a wrenching gift that seemed no less to me than the one Sarah made when she allowed Abraham to take Isaac into the desert as a sacrifice to God. But unlike Sarah, I knew my son would live forever in the presence of the Lord, and so I took solace in this. I spent every moment with him, and Elkanah gladly indulged me, wanting nothing more than my contentment.

From the time Samuel was an infant, I spoke to him of the Lord, the God of Israel. Even as he suckled, his eyes still unopened, I whispered to him about how he was a special child, given and chosen by the Lord. Even as his tiny hands clenched and his pretty feet kicked, I told him how he would go to live with the Lord and serve him. Even when his dark hair was no more than soft wisps upon the crown of his head, I crooned songs, which I made up by the moment, of how blessed he was to be so well-loved by both his mother and the Lord.

Peninnah ridiculed me unmercifully for this, but I ignored her, and later, as I continued to speak so to my son, she left off in disgruntled uncertainty. For it surely appeared even to her that Samuel comprehended my meaning, and he heard my soft words of his fate with what seemed to my loving agreement.

When I had weaned Samuel, we went up to Shiloh. Can anyone imagine the transcendent ecstasy as it mixed with excruciating grief in the very well of my body and soul? The unutterable joy was in the perfect gift God had made to me of Samuel; the piercing sorrow was not so much in the giving back of that gift, for I had promised as much, but in the loss of the boy in my daily life. I had come to fashion my whole life around him, and he was his mother's joy as I imagined no son had been since the beginning of time. I'd delighted in watching his antics, took physical pleasure in his suckling, laughed aloud at his smile, celebrated his first steps, and counted every finger and toe each morning when I awoke. He had been the fulfillment of all my yearning, and he'd become the living symbol of all that was good in my life.

And now I must give him up.

Elkanah was uncharacteristically silent on the way to Shiloh, attending the young bull and other sacrifices we brought to offer the Lord. I knew my husband feared how I would fare once at the house of the Lord, whether I would be able to turn over our son...whether I even should. I knew he wondered how I would survive if I kept my vow. Surely he dreaded the joy and light draining out of our home at Ramah if Samuel was left in the house of the Lord.

The same questions troubled my heart; except one: I never doubted whether I should turn my son over to the priests at Shiloh. He'd been a gift from God and was due back to the giver. In that, I would never truly lose him for he had, from the beginning, belonged to the Lord and to me. In this I took comfort for I'd learned the one vital lesson: The Lord would sustain me now as he had in the past.

Once at Shiloh, we slaughtered the bull and offered our sacrifices. I saw Eli watching me and I came forward, crying out, "As you live, my lord, I am the woman who was standing here in your presence, praying to the Lord. For this child I prayed; and the Lord has granted me the petition that I made to him. Therefore as long as he lives, he is given to the Lord." Without speaking, Eli took Samuel in his arms. Samuel, though a young child, did not struggle or cry out. As I retreated and left that place, his dark, solemn eyes stayed fixed upon me, but he did not utter a sound of dismay or protest.

I knew then, as I turned from him lest he see my tears and know his mother was weaker than he, that he had indeed understood the words I'd spoken of the Lord from his infancy. Whether my tears that flowed during the whole trip back to Ramah were of grief or joy I cannot say, even now.

I know only that it was in the throes of such transporting emotion that I sang a prayer which seemed a living thing, forming in my mind even as I proclaimed it, "My heart exults in the Lord; my strength is exalted in my God. My mouth derides my enemies because I rejoice in my victory...There is no holy one like the Lord, no one besides you; there is no rock like our God. Talk no more so very proudly, let not arrogance come from your mouth; for the Lord is a God of knowledge, and by him actions are weighed...the barren has borne seven, but she who has many children is forlorn. The Lord kills and brings to life; he brings low, he also exalts. He raises up the poor from the dust; he lifts the needy from the ash heap, to make them sit with princes and inherit a seat of honor."

Peninnah's face darkened in rage and shame when I finished my song, and this pleased me, though I am not proud of this. Only later, when Samuel's fate and purpose to the Lord became known, did I come to understand the true meaning of the words I'd sung and whence they'd come. The Lord had given me this song, but not in order to humiliate Peninnah, as I'd so foolishly assumed. The Lord does not seek to shame, and it was no credit to me that I spoke his words with such low intent.

As it came to pass, the prayer I was given in those exalted moments was less a rebuke of Peninnah than a prophecy of what my son, Samuel, would become to the Lord. For at that time, Eli was the high priest, but his sons, Hophni and Phinehas, were evil men. Though also priests by the ancestry of their father, they did ill in the eyes of the Lord and in the company of the people. Their disrespect to their father and to the Lord, the God of Israel, knew no bounds, even unto stealing from the sacrifices made to the Lord and lying with serving woman at the entrance to the tent of meeting. Such were horrible abominations in Israel, and the people turned away from the house of Eli.

And I myself mourned greatly, for my beloved Samuel was serving Eli at that time, and I wondered what might become of him. Still, I did not interfere, though Peninnah whispered that a good, loving mother would certainly fetch her son back from men who treated the offerings and place of the Lord with such contempt. Yet I had faith in the Lord, and kept my vow to him. I knew as well that Eli was a good man who mourned the debauchery and disrespect of his sons, though he seemed unable to chastise them.

I also knew that Samuel flourished, for every year when Elkanah and I went to Shiloh to offer sacrifice, I visited my son. My only gift to him, year after year, was a robe I made with my own hands, putting all my loss and longing and love into each stitch. Samuel was much favored in Eli's eyes, and Eli, perhaps thinking of the disgrace of his own sons, blessed Elkanah and me, saying, "May the Lord repay you with children by this woman for the gift that she made to the Lord." And thus, the Lord consoled me for the loss of Samuel, for in each of the five years that Eli gave us this blessing, I conceived. I bore three more sons and two daughters. Not once did I complain in the agonies of childbirth or in the labor of caring for five young children. I remembered how Peninnah would whine and sigh of her exhaustion in childbearing and raising, but I never spoke one word of discontent. Would a woman who'd been starved for years complain of the food she was finally given?

Samuel remained in Shiloh, growing up in the presence of the Lord. And no matter what I heard regarding the sons of Eli, I trusted to God to protect and nurture my son.

My faith in God was rewarded. Disgusted by the sons of Eli, the Lord turned away from the house of Eli. Seldom was his word heard in Shiloh anymore, nor were visions given as often as of old. And after this time, it was told by a certain man of God that the Lord's favor had been finally riven from the house of Eli, and that another would be raised up to serve the Lord. Shortly after this, Samuel heard the call of the Lord as he slept in the temple. The Lord told Samuel that the prophecy was true: the Lord intended to punish Eli's house forever by removing his favor.

Samuel, my kind young son, was afraid to tell this vision to Eli. But Eli insisted, and when he'd heard the words of the Lord as spoken to my boy, Samuel, he accepted the decree.

From that day forth, Samuel grew in strength and grace before the Lord at Shiloh and before all of Israel. And as his power in the Lord increased, the words of my prophecy were fulfilled. Indeed, in Samuel, the Lord did bring low and exalt, he did kill and bring to life. Not only did God raise a lowly boy, one given to a seemingly barren mother, to become the most powerful judge of Israel, he empowered this his lowly boy, this nazirite, to anoint kings. And those kings, both Saul and David, were raised and brought low during the days and according to the words of Samuel. My son.

Active Meditation

Hannah, even as she prayed unceasingly for a son, prayed in a "surrendered" manner; in the same breath that she pleaded for a son, she offered that same son to God. Her very prayer was a surrender to God's power, God's will. Do we pray in such a way? Do we offer God the results and the benefits we will receive when he answers our prayer at the very same time that we make the prayer? If we examined our prayer lives, would we discover never-ending lists of needs, wishes, desires, even demands? Do we stop to give thanks for answered prayers?

Beginning today, focus on making at least one daily prayer in a "surrendered" manner. Start simply: when praying for something you normally pray for—i.e., healing of a physical or mental malady—make sure you willingly "surrender" the results of your prayer to God. Using the example of healing, this prayer might sound like this: "Dear Lord, I pray that you heal my cancer. I thank you for the good people I've met during the challenge of this disease. I thank you for the lessons I've learned. And I pledge to continue seeking you and your will for me in this process. I put my healing and my life in your hands, Lord, and I ask. You to lead me to use my health and my illness according to your will. After you fashion your own surrendered prayer, repeat some version of it daily, and, eventually, try to apply it to all your prayers.

Reflection/Discussion Questions

1. Do you prefer to pray alone or in a community? Why?

2. Do you feel that God answers your prayers? How do you know?

3. How do you feel about the kind of "charismatic" praying that involves physical, public, and emotional proclamations?

4. Do you have a particular place where you like to pray?

5. How do you explain it when someone prays fervently and doesn't receive the answer she or he deeply desires?

CHAPTER VIII

Abigail

Wit and wisdom

I SAMUEL, CHAPTERS 25—26

When I was young, I fell in love with a fool. In that, I am not so different from most women. Later, I married a king. For that, I am celebrated worldwide for my wisdom. As far as I'm concerned, it was just a matter of learning from my mistakes.

Looking back, I'd like to say I can't imagine why I fell in love with my first husband. It would make me sound so much more sensible and discerning than I really was. It would be like what people in your world call "pleading the fifth." I could deny all knowledge of what possessed me in order to avoid incriminating myself. But the simple truth is I know precisely why I fell in love with Nabal.

He was loud and brash and rich and handsome. And I was quiet and uncertain and poor and ugly. Or so I thought. My mother had assured me from childhood that I "would never attract men like locusts." For as long as I could remember, she had suggested I "win a man with honey, because you certainly won't do it with your face and figure." By the time Nabal came blustering into my life, I was only fifteen years old, but I was utterly convinced that I would never marry: no man could possibly want someone as plain and shy as I. After all, my childhood friends were married, some for years! There had to be something wrong with me. My mother was surely correct in her assessment.

I hasten to add that my mother loved me dearly. And I'm not just saying that out of some misguided sense of loyalty or any lack of confidence. I gave all that up too long ago to measure. No, I know she loved me and wanted the best for me. For her, giving me the best meant preparing me for modesty and as good a marriage as she could arrange. And this involved making certain that I did not think too well of myself. Her mother had done the same to her, and my great-grandmother had done the same to her, and on and on as far back as memory might serve. This is simply how it was done among the women in my mother's line. It was many years before I understood that I did, indeed, possess a degree of beauty. My mother would have never dreamt of telling me so.

Today, her behavior might be called cruel or even abusive, and given the result—a tongue-tied, paralyzed daughter who felt compelled to accept the first offer of marriage that came her way—perhaps such characterizations would not be far wrong. But this is now, and that was then. Then, no one thought anything amiss in such tactics. In fact, my mother was revered in our village as a strong, cunning matron who managed to marry off seven daughters with nary a protest from one of us. We didn't dare. And for those who might think my husband bad, well, they should have seen the slugs several of my sisters were forced to accept. More than once I saw one particular sister wearing ugly bruises on her face and arms, and I can recall hearing another's sobs as she recounted her wedding night.

At least I loved Nabal. Or so I thought. He was what many might call a loudmouth or know-it-all, but I was awed by his presence. He always seemed to have something to say, and whatever it was, he said it with conviction and in no weak voice. He was larger than life, handsome, I thought at the time, equating his size with power and bearing. Truth is, he ran to fat which I might have observed, even at the tender age of fifteen, had I not been blinded by my abiding desire to marry someone! And Nabal was no small catch from my mother's perspective, and therefore, mine. Not only was he a remarkable, if somewhat noisy, presence, he'd already inherited significant properties and herds from his father.

And he was barely thirty years old, which was quite an improvement over the last husband my mother had selected for my sister Maela: a shrunken fifty-nine-year-old goat herder, wrinkled and darkened by the sun, whose profession always accompanied him in the odor that seemed to cling to his very skin. Maela had sobbed and begged to be allowed to reject the putrid-smelling old man, but my mother had been adamant, observing that the man was rich and would probably not live long anyway. My father, who was largely silent, seemed on the verge of rescuing Maela, but even as he took the rare deep breath that signified he was about to speak, my mother glared at him meaningfully. He exhaled a sigh and gave my sister an apologetic pat on the head as he quickly left the house.

So Nabal looked like a prince among men to me, but my two younger sisters, the only ones left at home, could not abide his over-bearing nature. They teased me unmercifully for my obvious infatuation, "Even his name names him a fool," for that was one interpretation of "Nabal." But my mother, after cuffing them none too gently, countered sternly, "The only fool would be one who turns away an offer of marriage from such a rich and powerful man."

My breath stopped. This was the first I'd heard of Nabal offering marriage. Oh I knew he'd been hanging about, and more than once I'd felt his eye on me at the well or in the village as I shopped for the day's meal, but I was much too shy and unconfident to imagine he might actually be considering me as a prospective wife. I stared at my mother in astonishment as my sisters cowered in the corner, nursing their wounds and muttering against our mother. Paying them no attention, she gave me a rare smile and an even rarer embrace, telling me, "Abigail, my beauty, you will marry well, perhaps better than any one of your sisters." And then she went out to finalize the arrangements. I had heard nothing beyond her calling me "my beauty," and those words echoed in my ears for weeks until the day I married.

I soon learned that Nabal was not the great prize my mother—and I—had thought. his seeming confidence was nothing more than loud arrogance; what had looked to be his muscular body was actually so much well-dressed fat; and what had seemed a strong character was really ill-tempered surliness. His wealth was real enough. My mother had made sure of that; she and my father lived long and well off the bride price Nabal had paid for me. But it was wealth unearned, for Nabal did not like well to work, and he drove his servants and workers cruelly. He squeezed every bit of strength and dignity from them, treating them much like the herds some of them tended in his stead. They were no different to him than the thousand goats and the three thousand sheep he called his own. It was all the same to Nabal: land, goats, sheep, servants, workers, wife. All nothing but property. His property.

Perhaps I had learned more from my mother than I knew, for I soon came to an accommodation with my husband. As the years passed, I learned to make him happy while keeping him out of my bed and away from my table as often as possible. This did not prove as difficult as may be imagined, for Nabal was not the brightest of men. Nothing more than a little subtlety, an occasional good meal, and a great deal of wine were required to keep my loutish husband content. I soon learned that the wine went far toward easing my role in bed: I needed only plead the necessity of setting the house in order or cleaning up after the meal, and he was often fast asleep by the time I came to bed.

There was never a cross word between us. I saw to that. And so, my life was not so bad, particularly as the years passed and I gently convinced Nabal that he was much more needed on his property than in our home. We had settled at his home in Maon when first we married, but his land and herds were mostly in Carmel. After the first year passed, I began to quietly suggest that he needed to be among his herds and properties in order to protect his growing wealth. I mentioned how an important land-owner like himself should surely be seen by the people to be managing his fortune, for how else would he gain their esteem and loyalty if not by his presence?

I nearly sabotaged my own efforts, though, by making our home in Maon too comfortable for him. He was waited on hand-and-foot by our house servants, and I was constantly there to flatter and ply him with wine. I didn't realize my error until I made the second annual visit to my mother's house. No longer the obedient daughter who hung on her every word and cringed lest I make her unhappy, I spoke frankly to her of my desire to have my husband out of our home as frequently as I could arrange it. As I described all my clever efforts to convince him to spend the greater share of the year on his property, she interrupted me, "And what do you provide him in your home that even his vanity cannot bear to part from?"

I immediately comprehended her meaning, but after thinking on it for a moment, I asked, "Am I to make my home a misery so to drive him out?"

Rolling her eyes, she snorted derisively. "Have you learned nothing from me, child? The man has untold wealth. See that he has a dwelling in Carmel that is as welcoming as the one you've made in Maon. That, combined with the belief you've planted in his heart that he must be more oft present on his lands will work upon him to your advantage."

Even now, with my renown for wisdom, I don't think I ever surpassed my mother in cunning.

I did as she suggested, traveling for a time with my husband to his land in Carmel where I oversaw the construction of a comfortable, nay luxurious by the measure of those days, abode. I insured that it boasted comforts lacking at my home in Maon, knowing how well he loved indulgence. During that time I came to know many of his young men and servants, and whenever my husband was absent, I treated them with kindness and generosity. Shortly I had won their allegiance, and though none dared complain to me of Nabal, I could see how they detested and feared him. I grieved for them and made sure to give them what I could of coin and extra food whenever possible. Nabal was well-pleased with his new house in Carmel and preened himself mightily before the local population and those who labored daily to finish the "master's dwelling."

When Nabal, accompanying me back to Maon after the dwelling in Carmel was finished, declared that he must return immediately and live out most of the year on his property as "a proper landowner of my wealth should," I made no remark. I felt no need to claim his thought as my own; I'd attained the end I sought. But I had learned in my time at Carmel that several of my women servants in Maon were married to Nabal's shepherds and laborers in Carmel. My sweet, sensitive husband had thought nothing of separating these couples for all but a few weeks of each year, and I determined to end this unthinking cruelty. I convinced him that he would need female servants to keep his house in Carmel, since I, of course, could not leave our home to live there. Pleased at the idea of arriving in state with new servants to run his household, he immediately agreed, telling me brusquely, "You select the maids; I have no time for such nonsense."

As if I'd any intention of letting him.

So, when he returned to Carmel, I sent with him the wives of men I'd met there, and my heart was the lighter in seeing their joy at the prospect of being reunited with their husbands. It was probably the only thing that could have made them eager to serve my husband. .

During those times, Samuel, the great prophet chosen by the Lord God of Israel, died, and all the nation mourned. Shortly after his burial in the place where Hannah had borne him in Ramah, Samuel's chosen prince, David, came down into our region, wandering the wilds of Paran in grief for Samuel and in avoidance of his avowed enemy, King Saul. David's presence was an unexpected boon for my husband's many herds for David's soldiers protected Nabal's shepherds and young men. Unlike many roving bands of soldiers and warriors, they never molested our young men or plundered the sheep and goats, and thus, Nabal's wealth and the peace of the region increased under David's watch.

In Nabal's frequent absence, my life also took on a peaceful nature. I welcomed the gentle routine of working our gardens and running the household with the few women I'd retained. Nabal often sent his young men to bring me some bounty and assure himself that I continued to keep his house and reputation safely. But that was of little import to me, and indeed, I welcomed hearing the news of the region from the young men. My sisters visited as often as they could, mostly for respite from their own husbands, and I took secret joy in providing them this haven. Though I delighted greatly in the children of my sisters and those of my young men and women, I considered it no great sorrow that I had none of my own. After all, I'd aided many a midwife in the births at Maon and Carmel and was never without a child running in and out of my home, or bouncing on my knee if I wished. And truth to tell, I'd come to consider my husband as nothing more than a large child; indeed, sometimes managing him was the same as if I'd had ten incorrigible sons. I had much to thank the Lord for: my life was full of pleasure and, most blessedly, peace.

I knew peace until the day one of Nabal's young men, whom I'd befriended during my days in Carmel, arrived breathless and full of dismay at my door. I urged him to recover himself with food and rest, but he insisted upon first speaking with me. His words froze the very heat of the desert, leaving my heart and bones shivering with cold and dread.

"David sent messengers out of the wilderness to salute our master," began the young man, his breath still ragged, "Our master shouted insults at them. Yet the men were very good to us, and we suffered no harm, and we never missed anything when we were in the fields as long as we were with them. Now therefore know this and consider what you should do; for evil has been decided against our master and against all his house; he is so ill-natured that no one can speak to him."

No one knew that better than I. I was horrified when the messenger described how David had only asked for a few provisions, provisions that David and his men had, in fact, protected for Nabal, and that Nabal had responded with the vilest of insults. David, upon hearing of it, had vowed to destroy Nabal and every man in his service. For one instant my anger blazed so intensely against my literal fool of a husband, I considered letting David take his revenge. Was it more than Nabal so richly deserved? It was only the thought of all those who must perish with him for his folly that moved me to action.

Instructing my young men to load our beasts with two hundred loaves, two skins of wine, five dressed sheep ready for the fire, five measures of parched grain, one hundred clusters of raisins, and two hundred cakes of figs, I mounted and rode on under the cover of the mountain. There, I espied David, armed with his troops to slaughter my husband and my beloved servants, coming toward me. As he was nigh, I leapt from my donkey, fell to the ground and cried:

"Upon me alone, my lord, be the guilt; please let your servant speak in your ears, and hear the words of your servant. My lord, do not take seriously this ill-natured fellow, Nabal; for as his name is, so is he; folly is with him;—(and so I echoed the judgment I'd so resented from my sisters years before)—but I, your servant, did not see the young men of my lord, whom you sent. Now then, my lord, as the Lord lives, and as you yourself live, since the Lord has restrained you from bloodguilt and from taking vengeance with your own hand, now let your enemies and those who seek to do evil to my lord be like Nabal. And now let this present that your servant has brought to my lord be given to the young men who follow my lord. Please forgive the trespass of your servant; for the Lord will certainly make my lord a sure house, because my lord is fighting the battles of the Lord; and evil shall not be found in you so long as you live…but the lives of your enemies he shall sling out as from the hollow of a sling."

I thought the reference to David's celebrated victory over Goliath was particularly clever. But when I continued, I cannot say I intended to end my speech as I did; yet it must have occurred to me that in all I was doing to protect Nabal's life and property, I might at least mention myself. Was it my prophecy of sorts? Or a prediction I might make happen? Who can say? Nonetheless, I added:

"And when the Lord has dealt well with my lord, then remember your servant."

During my pretty plea, David's rage had slowly been transformed to astonishment. I saw it writ large in his face and eyes when I finally dared look up. He stared hard at me for long moments, and after raising me, observed me even more closely before he spoke. I knew before he'd uttered one word that he liked what he'd seen—and heard, of course—and that my husband's people would be spared. During that breathless moment when my eyes met those of Samuel's anointed one, I did not think of Nabal at all.

David responded like the king he would become, graciously accepting the gifts I'd brought and promising to turn aside his wrath so that it would not harm me or my household. "Blessed be the Lord, the God of Israel who sent you to meet me today!" he proclaimed, "Blessed be your good sense, and blessed be you, who have kept me today from bloodguilt and from avenging myself by my own hand! Go up to your house in peace; I have heeded your voice, and I have granted your petition."

I confess that relief warred with a sense of deep loss as I watched him ride away with his men. What must it be like to have such a man? I stood for some time, staring after him, until one of my servants gently reminded me we must return. Left unsaid was his fear that I must now deal with his master, my husband, Nabal. The fool.

We did not return to Maon, for I had resolved to teach him a lesson, and so we journeyed to Carmel. I could tell our young men were full of trepidation at my unspoken intent, but I would not be turned back. They worried that Nabal would be enraged that I had given David so much from our stores, but I was beyond any such trivial concern. My husband had risked not only his own worthless life, but mine and the life of all the servants and young men and women who depended upon us. And I would make certain he knew of the disaster I had averted.

Not surprisingly, he was in the midst of a drunken feast when I arrived. I knew well that this was how he spent much of his time "overseeing" his property, but I had little care for such things; I was merely grateful that I was not forced to be in presence. However I was not going to make what I had to say any easier by telling him while he was too merrily drunk to comprehend. Thus I settled in for the night, and waiting until well after dawn the next day, went in to him. Without raising my voice, I gave him the stark details of what had transpired. I left out nothing, including David's vow that he would have destroyed all men of the household of Nabal had I not intervened.

All the color drained out of my husband's fleshy face. He was already feeling poorly, the sour smell of too much wine hung about him, but my words set him trembling. Though he'd made no attempt to rise to greet me when I'd entered, now he fell back onto his unkempt bed, staring at me in horror. The full import of what had occurred fell upon him with no wine to mitigate its impact. He opened his mouth to speak, but could do nothing more than gasp heavily as he envisioned his own death at the hands of Samuel's outlaw prince. I did not imagine that he spent one moment considering the destruction he'd nearly brought upon our people and our lands. I knew he spared no such thought, consumed as he was with himself. Without another word I left him thus, his mouth working convulsively as he clutched the bedclothes about him.

I stayed in Carmel for the next ten days, comforting our people and conducting the business of our properties. Nabal was useless, his heart having turned to stone within him at my words. He did not leave his bed-chamber from the morning I'd brought him the news of David. I cared for him as best I could, bringing him broth and cleaning him and sitting with him as he fitfully slept. None may say I was not a dutiful wife.

On the tenth day, the Lord struck him and he died, having never recovered his speech. I sent one of my young men to David to report what had befallen Nabal, and my servant returned to report that David had proclaimed, "Blessed be the Lord, who has judged the case of Nabal's insult, and has kept back his servant from evil; the Lord has returned the evildoing of Nabal upon his own head."

Nor was this David's last word on the matter. When a suitable time had passed, he sent to me, through his servants, asking me to become his wife. Imagining what my mother would say—"Only a fool would surrender control of such property and wealth to marry a hunted out-law wandering in the wilds"—I smiled within myself and immediately agreed. On that very day, I rose and, taking five of my maids, rode out to meet my new husband.

It is true that I did not mourn Nabal overlong. I had been a good and loyal wife to him, and he had been a selfish, surly husband. Only by using his vanity to manage him had I created a respectable life for myself. He had abused our servants and nearly squandered all our prop-erty. The Lord had chosen between him and David; so had I.

There has been much debate about me over the centuries and the millennia. Was I wise, or was I deceitful? A good wife, or a manipulative whore? Witty, or wily? Sensible, or greedy? None of this is of any account to me; nor does the judgment of any person touch me. I mere-ly did what successful men and women have done since time immemo-rial: I used the skills and talents I had to my advantage. I lived with the consequences and I accepted the rewards of my actions.

I can only declare that before the one judge who matters to me.

Active Meditation

No matter how determined we are to mind our own business or avoid co-dependency, we all have "Abigail moments," those times when we wholeheartedly believe that our failure to act on behalf of someone close to us will result in serious, perhaps even fatal, consequences. It could be a child on drugs, an aging parent who is endangering herself, a spouse who is clinically depressed and unable to act, a friend trapped in an abusive relationship. These and countless other situations are excruciatingly difficult to live through, never mind to act upon. There are no easy answers. However, consider these concrete steps to help confront and resolve very difficult decisions:

1. Prayer. Pour out your fears and ask God for guidance, trusting that he provides it even if you don't "hear" a clear answer at first.
2. Seek professional advice. There are myriad sources of help for those in need: Alcoholics Anonymous. Al Anon. Suicide hotlines. Federal, state and local government sponsored physical and mental health programs. Local hospitals. Counselors. School guidance departments. All—and many more—can be found in local phone books.
3. Talk to your doctor if this is a medical issue.
4. Talk to your faith advisor.
5. Ask yourself what Jesus, who lived among and loved men and women, would do.

Reflection/Discussion Questions

1. Have you ever intervened in a situation involving someone close to you and regretted it?
2. If you believe someone close to you is incapable of making a decision to help themselves, are you obligated to make that decision for them?
3. How do you define co-dependency? Have you experienced it in your own life?
4. If you were facing a difficult issue involving someone close to you, would your first resource be your faith advisor? Why or why not?
5. Have you ever intervened in a situation involving someone close to you and felt rewarded by your action?

CHAPTER IX

The Shunemmitess

Generosity rewarded

2 KINGS, CHAPTERS 2—8

I can't say what instinct prompted me to take a homeless stranger and his companion into my home. I can only say that I never regretted it.

After all, isn't that what the Lord, the God of Israel, asks of us? That we shelter and feed the stranger? That we welcome the one who is unwelcome elsewhere? That we protect the unprotected? That we succor the needy? This is all I did, really.

My neighbors thought I was crazy, and so, I imagine, did my family and friends. Certainly, they resented my actions, fearing that I would bring them in contact with unsavory characters. I'm sure they spoke ill of me in my absence. But no one dared speak so in my presence.

I had money.

So I did as I pleased and paid no heed to what anyone said or thought. The homeless preacher, Elisha, and his companion, Gehazi, weren't the first to receive my attention. I was always on the watch for travelers who needed a meal or money, or just someone to listen to their stories. What good is wealth if one can't use it to do good? I enjoyed my converse with these wanderers and often learned much of the surrounding world and its many ways. Though no one may believe it, I received more than I gave.

But from the first, there was something different about Elisha. For one thing, he never asked for a gift—not even a morsel of food; nor did he seek my attention. By the time he came into our region, many a traveler had heard of me and some would come seeking a meal or some few coins to ease their way. Yet Elisha never sought me out, and that alone might have awakened my interest. It was I who eventually sought him.

I knew he passed often through Shunem, our village, and upon occasion I watched him pass by with Gehazi. There was nothing particularly attractive about Elisha; in fact, quite the contrary: he was bald and ungainly, always wearing a grim, somber expression. His garb was humble and often soiled by his days of travel. Still, there was something compelling about the man. Though he was a stranger to our village, his reputation as a miracle-worker and counselor to kings had preceded him. I'd heard word of him through the many travelers and strangers who'd eaten at my table or accepted my gifts.

Though known for his temper, he was considered by many to be the spiritual heir of the great Elijah, whom he'd served for many years. Indeed, it was said that Elisha had stood by and watched as his mentor Elijah was taken into heaven in a whirlwind of fire and heavenly chariots. At that moment, Elijah himself had willed his spirit, doubling it even in strength, to Elisha; and from then on, kings had feared to offend the stern student who'd assumed twice the strength of his master. And yet, Elisha was also known for extreme kindness. It was told that a poor widow of one of his fellow prophets had been destitute and about to lose her children to slave-drivers. She appealed to him, and Elisha had caused fine oil to flow and be gathered into vessels until there was so much that she could sell enough to pay her debts and keep a living for her and her children. But few in Shunem knew such things for certain; they were only rumors brought to me on the lips of other itinerants.

I decided to find out for myself. One day when Elisha was passing through Shunem, I went out myself and appealed to him, pressing him to dine at my table. I did not send one of my many servants, nor did I ask my good-hearted husband to go. I went myself, and perhaps for that reason, the man agreed. I knew long before that meal was finished that Elisha, despite his solemn ways and temperament, was an extraordinary man. He seldom spoke directly to us, often speaking through his servant, Gehazi, though we all sat together at table. This may strike some as arrogance, but in Elisha it seemed more to protect us from the terrifying power of God who spoke through the prophet and resided in spirit with him. After all, Elisha had once used the name of the Lord to curse some boys who were teasing him, and immediately, two bears had come out of the nearby woods and mauled the children! Such a man, who lives so utterly in the shadow of the power of God, soon learns to shield those he wishes to protect. Thus, we became friends of a sort, as much as anyone can be friends with a prophet, and whenever he came through Shunem, he ate at our table. He trusted me, and that meant more than I could even comprehend at the time. The whispers of neighbors and villagers meant nothing.

I know they questioned how my husband could allow me to court such a friendship. No doubt, they'd mocked my husband for years, hissing that I would waste all his wealth on strangers and dirty travelers. But he was a man kind and good even beyond his advanced years, and he never looked askance at me. Never once did he demand that I conduct myself with more reticence or cultivate more appropriate companions. If he heard the gossip, and I'm sure word came to him, for people love to stir the pot, he never said a word of it to me.

And it wasn't only because when we'd married, I'd added my own money to his already considerable store of wealth. It wasn't because he was an old man, as I know they said, addled by the beauty and wiles of a younger wife. It wasn't because he spent much of his time working in our fields and encouraging our young men and women, though he did. It wasn't because I kept our household running impeccably and saw to his every comfort, though I did.

No, it was simply because he was a good man who loved me and wished to indulge me in whatever enterprise heartened me and nourished my spirit. If that enterprise was charity, equally given to all in need regardless of status or state of cleanliness, then so be it. A pious man who knew the will of God better than most who claimed to be priests, my husband would not stint in allowing me to be generous as the Lord commanded we must.

Still, there was perhaps another reason why he supported my will in all things, though we never once spoke of it. I'd borne no child, even after years of marriage, and I think he knew the emptiness in my soul. It was not only that I yearned for a babe to nurse at my breast and hold in my arms, but even more, I longed to give this beloved man who was so good a child. Our child. We had none, and he was growing old. These words never passed between us. Surely he must have wanted a child, born of our deep love, but not once did I hear resentment or recriminations from his lips. Indeed, all I ever heard from him was the soft language of love and encouragement in everything I did.

And this made me wish all the more to bear us a child.

Oh, I was not fool enough to think that entertaining the poor and itinerant was a substitute for motherhood. The two were very different, each valuable in its way, and I knew that as well as my husband did. But pursuing the one did at least fill the emptiness left by the other's absence, and so my dear, good man urged me to open our home and coffers as I saw fit.

So when I told him we should build a roof-top chamber for Elisha, he merely smiled and told me to do as I wished. "Look," I said, thinking I should at least provide some explanation for this extraordinary plan, "I am sure that this man is a holy man of God." Before I could continue, he raised his hand, rose from our table and came around to embrace me. He told me I did not need his permission, but if I wanted it, I certainly had it in this as in all things.

Then he went out to our lands. And I wept.

But not for long. Soon I was busy with carpenters and furniture makers and builders. The rooftop chamber, though simple, looked magnificent on the top of our dwelling. It was high enough for Elisha to see his beloved Mount Carmel where he often went to pray and preach. I took great pleasure in imagining the grumblings of my neighbors as this structure progressed. I made sure everyone knew it was for the stern prophet and his servant, and this caused a great deal of turmoil, much to my delight. By then, all had heard of the exploits of Elisha, and few wanted such a powerful and untenable prophet living in such close proximity. Many of the villagers were disconcerted about the lofty height of his eyrie, knowing full well he would be able to see all that went on below him. Not all those who gossiped so freely about me were proud of their own conduct, and it dismayed them greatly to think they would be living under the all-seeing eyes of such a frightening prophet.

I must confess I oft found myself laughing aloud at their distress. And this, of course, did little to endear me to those who already mistrusted me. I was by then considered what the people of your world would call an eccentric, and I admit I very much enjoyed this status. In this, I think, I was not so very generous...or charitable.

The chamber was soon finished: whatever they might say of me, my money was good and I employed more than a few laborers from our village. We welcomed Elisha and Gehazi with no great ceremony, and the prophet took easily to his new abode, staying with us whenever he was in the region. Though his appreciation was evident—where else could such a prophet truly rest and be comforted by peace and solitude?—he offered no formal thanks; nor did we want or expect such a thing.

But what he did offer me was of a value beyond any thanks or price I could have named.

Not long after he'd accepted our gift of sanctuary, he sent Gehazi to summon me to his chamber. When I followed Gehazi into the room where Elisha was resting, I could feel the strong presence of God around the prophet. My sense was confirmed when Elisha began to speak to me through Gehazi, as was his wont when the Lord was close by. I had only heard of Elisha's many miracles—both kind and terrifying—and I was excited, wondering if I would be witness to some nearby miracle. How could I have imagined precisely how nearby that miracle would be?

But at that time, there was no sign of wonders or miracles. Elisha merely directed Gehazi to ask me if there was anything the prophet could do for us in recompense for building his chamber. Using Elisha's words, Gehazi asked, "Would you have a word spoken on your behalf to the king or the commander of the army?"

Perhaps a little offended at having my generosity so named, or more likely disappointed that this was to be a mere matter of offering repayment with no evident miracle, I replied somewhat haughtily, "I live among my own people," thus communicating in no uncertain terms that I was powerful in my own right and did not need his intervention with the leaders of my land.

Elisha was silent, and I departed, a little irritated by the exchange. What passed in my absence between Elisha and his much more sensitive servant, Gehazi, I can only guess at from what came next. I had no sooner returned downstairs then did Gehazi return for me, saying that his master wished to see me again. I was about to protest when the servant took my hand and looked into my face without speaking. I followed him silently.

When we'd returned to Elisha, I stayed at the entrance, not entering his room. This time he spoke directly to me: "At this season, in due time, you shall embrace a son."

All the air—and the ire—went out of me, and I could hardly draw breath. How had he learned of my most concealed desire? I had known him to be a man of God, but was he truly so blessed a prophet as to discern the secrets of a soul? I instinctively wrapped my arms around myself, as though to shield me from the gaping wound that such a promise, unkept, must rend. And betraying my lack of faith, I cried, "Oh no, my lord, O man of God; do not deceive your servant."

But he had not deceived me. Nor had he discerned my yearning on his own: I learned later from a servant who'd overheard the exchange that Gehazi had suggested to Elisha that the only thing my husband and I lacked was a son. Elisha may have been a prophet, but his servant was a pragmatist. And by that season in the following year, I held my babe in my arms, though I could hardly keep him there, for my husband, ever joyful, would hardly be parted from his son. Was any child more cherished from the day Isaac was born to Sarah?

When he wasn't being held and suckled by his mother, he was the constant companion of his father and the beloved tyrant among our household servants who could deny him nothing. Even Elisha, who was certainly not known for his love of little children, seemed pleasantly surprised by the boy, as though the very prophet who'd promised his birth hadn't expected such a happy result. And my son, a lovely outgoing child who chattered constantly, could occasionally be found sitting silently with the prophet in his chambers, as though the boy comprehended the man's need for peace. They made quite a comical pair in those moments, the child unconsciously assuming the pose and demeanor of Elisha, as if to show his respect by reflection.

As soon as he was old enough, our son began to accompany his father into the fields, though I suspect it was less for the son to learn the family business than it was for the father to entertain the son! Still, the delight they took in one another, and I in them, brought a warmth and joy to our lives that we'd never imagined possible.

And then one day, a servant carried my son home from the fields, and when I saw the child's face, my heart stopped. He was flushed and feverish and moaning of pain in his head. I held him in my arms to calm and soothe him, but it did no good. He only worsened, his moans becoming mere whimpers as pain and exhaustion bore him away. At the noon hour he died in my embrace.

A resolve hardened in me like brick, and shedding no tears, I carried my son up to the prophet's rooms, ignoring the grief of my servants as they pleaded with me to let them help. But he was weightless in my arms as I laid him on the prophet's bed and left, closing the door firmly behind me. Then I sent to my husband, but not to break his heart with news of the death that would surely cause his own. No, instead I sent to him asking for a servant and donkey so that I could quickly go to the holy man who was then on Mount Carmel. My husband, not understanding what had happened, wondered why I wished to go to Elisha so hurriedly. But I only replied, "It will be all right," and the dear man, accustomed to my whims, sent the servant and the donkey.

When I was nigh onto Mount Carmel, the sharp-eyed Elisha saw me coming and sent Gehazi to me immediately to inquire what was wrong that I should come to him so rapidly and at such a time. But I gave Gehazi the same answer I'd given my husband, "It will be all right," and I continued on, ignoring Gehazi. Through all this, my heart was like a stone set on only one thing: Elisha.

When I reached him, with Gehazi still hovering nearby, I fell on my face and caught hold of Elisha's feet. Gehazi moved to stop me, but

Elisha warned him away, "Let her alone, for she is in bitter distress; the Lord has hidden it from me and has not told me."

At these words the stone encasing my heart cracked just slightly for I thought to myself: if the Lord has hidden it from Elisha, then at least the prophet has not willed this death and may still offer hope. Thus I spoke plaintively to Elisha, "Did I ask my lord for a son? Did I not say, 'Do not mislead me'?"

Comprehension darkened the brow of the prophet and sorrow for my anguish filled his eyes. He immediately raised me up and gave his staff to Gehazi, instructing him to return immediately with me to Shunem and lay the staff on the face of the boy. But this was not what I had come for. It had not been Gehazi who had promised me a son, and so I told Elisha boldly, "As the Lord lives, and as you yourself live, I will not leave without you."

Gehazi went ahead to do as he was bid, but Elisha, who himself had loved my son as well as such a man was capable of loving a child, followed with me. He made no reply when Gehazi returned to meet us, saying that the child was still dead and had not stirred when the staff was laid upon him. Not another word passed between us as we continued, eventually entering the house and climbing up to Elisha's chamber where my son lay. There, he turned us away and entered, closing the door behind him. Only then did my heart's dam break and I sobbed, falling to my knees. Gehazi lifted me gently and brought me downstairs to wait.

What seemed an eternity, but was no more than fleeting moments, passed before Gehazi summoned me. I don't remember my feet on the steps, only that I was at the door of the chamber where Elisha met me. Gesturing inside, he said only, "Take your son." For the second time that day, I fell at the feet of the prophet, before rising to take my living son into my arms and bring him down into our home. Only after my husband had returned for the evening and held his son in his arms, marveling at how well he'd recovered from that morning's illness, did I tell him of the miracle.

This was not the last time Elisha preserved and protected my family. He continued to stay with us over the months and years, though as his reputation grew he was required to be away more frequently. His power in the service of the Lord grew with each passing day until the very kings and commanders courted his approval and dreaded his displeasure. Yet he was only kind to us, if often silent, and sought the peace of his chamber as often as he could.

Never again did I have to remind Elisha of his promise to me of a living son, and when the day came of the Lord's anger with his people, Elisha warned me, "Get up and go with your household, and settle wherever you can; for the Lord has called for a famine, and it will come on the land for seven years."

I took my household and my son and went into the region of the Philistines where we settled for the seven years while famine ravaged the land of Israel. Though we were strangers among the Philistines, our wealth served us well and we were treated with respect, if not for ourselves, for our money. It may be that even the Philistines feared the power of Elisha, for we were left unmolested, though we yearned for our home.

When we returned to our land after the famine, all was in chaos. Homes and lands that were abandoned because of the famine had been confiscated by the king and the commanders of the army. Returning landowners were at the mercy of whomever had taken their property, and many lost everything they had not taken with them into exile. Elisha had repaid my small kindness to him many times over, and I would not disrupt his work to ask for help now.

Instead, relying on my name and reputation, I dressed in my finery and set out myself with a caravan of servants and gifts to appeal directly to the king for my house and land. When I arrived at the king's palace, I was kept waiting because, as his servants told me proudly, "Our king is conversing with Gehazi, servant of the man of God."

I smiled to myself at the ways of life, but I would still not appeal to Gehazi for help. How could I ask for more when so much had already been given to me? And so I waited, but the servant must have gone in to the king and whispered that the wealthy Shunemmitess had returned from the land of the Philistines and was waiting to appeal for her property. Gehazi was even at that moment recounting to the king how Elisha had restored my son to life, and when Gehazi heard that I waited outside, he told the king that I was the very woman of whom they spoke.

The king, who much loved to hear stories showing the power of God's prophet, immediately brought me in and questioned me about how my son was restored to life. I affirmed Gehazi's words, and the king, perhaps fearing to offend Elisha by denying one whom the prophet so clearly loved, appointed an official to oversee my appeal. He told the man, "Restore all that was hers, together with all the revenue of the fields from the day that she left the land until now." And so once again, Elisha had saved us. Our wealth was restored twofold, and we regained everything we'd lost during the famine.

Had Elisha known what would transpire that day in the king's court? Had he deliberately sent Gehazi to converse with the king, knowing that only Gehazi's presence would ensure the restoration of my property? For me, there is no doubt. Let others debate.

One truth cannot be debated, or doubted. For one small kindness to one homeless man, I received untold and unasked for rewards. But the greatest among these was the only one I sought from the beginning: to know, perhaps better than anyone, the heart and mind of the great, strange prophet.

Active Meditation

The Shunemmitess stands out, not simply because she was generous, but because of the recipient of her generosity. She was not generous to a member of her family or even her community, and she was not even generous to a stranger who was nonetheless harmless and easy to please. No. She was generous to a stranger who also happened to be a loud, wild-eyed, unkempt preacher who frightened most people who encountered him.

How many of us could claim that our charity stretches so far? When we give our money, our time, or even our prayers, do we more often than not give to those we know, those who may share our beliefs, geography, culture? We may feel comfortable giving to the local soup kitchen, run by our church or a local government, but do we feel as comfortable contributing to a program that aids ex-convicts in returning to their communities? We may be happy to donate to AIDS research, but are we as quick to volunteer at an AIDS shelter or hospice?

Take this opportunity to "stretch" your charity beyond the familiar. Give time, money, and prayers in a way you never have before. Visit a convalescent home or hospice and spend time with a patient who seldom gets visitors. Give money or a bag of groceries to a panhandler or street person. Pray for Muslims who are oppressed and fearful throughout the world. The rewards from your new-found generosity may not be as evident as those of the Shunammitess, but they will surely come.

Reflection/Discussion Questions

1. Do you believe that "charity begins at home" and need not extend much further?
2. Do you focus more on giving money or time? Would you like to change that balance?
3. Have you ever rejected contributing to a charitable institution because "who knows how they really use the money?" without checking on the institution's record?
4. Does giving or "tithing" at your church erase your obligation to contribute elsewhere?
5. Are your charitable activities motivated primarily by the desire to improve this world or to attain the next? Or both?

CHAPTER X

Judith

Courage

JUDITH, CHAPTERS 1—16

When my husband died, I wanted to do nothing more than crawl into the tomb with him.

Manasseh was still young when he took ill working side-by-side with our people in our fields during the heat of the day. He came home to his bed and died there, thus ending my life and all my joy. People tried to comfort me, reminding me of the great wealth we'd accumulated during our marriage, of our property and estate, of my beautiful raiment and numerous jewels and finely worked gold. All this was as nothing to me.

Though our wedding was arranged and I'd never set eyes on Manasseh until the day we exchanged vows, ours became a loving marriage. In that I was blessed; many women were not so lucky. But Manasseh was a strong, good man; and though not overly given to expressions of affection, I knew his heart. And he knew mine. We prospered, as did our young men and women and servants. My husband was renowned for his fairness; often he would work as hard in the fields as our people. And I took my lessons from him, treating my maids and house servants with decency and respect, encouraging their worship of the Lord and helping their families. Our household and estate became like a small village within our city of Bethulia, and many envied us.

So after his death when well-meaning folk told me I must go on, I must think of all we'd built together, I made no reply. But my heart cried out in agony. What was wealth if we could not use it to ease our aging together? What was property if we could not visit it together, overseeing the harvests and healing of the land? What were raiment and jewels and gold if I could not wear it to please only his eyes? Nothing. Ashes. Death.

But death could not be mine. There was one alone whom I loved more than Manasseh, and he would not yet summon me into peaceful death, no matter how I wished it. The Lord, the God of Israel, had been my Lord and holy counsel all of my life, and he did not desert me when Manasseh was taken. Though I begged him to let me join my husband, to let my body die the way my spirit had, this was not the Lord's plan. It was his will that I live, and so, ashes and sackcloth and fasting became my life. I refused to remain in the beautiful house my husband had built for me, and instead, I insisted on setting up a tent on the roof of that home. My servants and relatives and friends protested greatly, but I would have it no other way. And when no one believed my desire, I put up the tent myself.

There I dwelled, tying sackcloth about my waist, dressing in widow's garb, and fasting always in adoration of the Lord. Other than my maid, one whom I particularly trusted because she understood me and had come with me to my husband's home, the Lord was my only companion. I broke my fast only on the prescribed days of the Lord: the day before the Sabbath, the Sabbath, the day before the new moon, the day of the new moon, and during Israel's festivals to the Lord. Even on those days, though I did not fast, I remained a widow in my heart and my dress.

Now, during the three years and four months of my widowhood I lived thus, a recluse, while great and terrible things were happening in the world. The pagan king of the Assyrians, Nebuchadnezzar, had conquered his most formidable enemy, Arphaxad, ruler of Medes, and was now moving, as it were, across the very world, in a campaign of vengeance and conquest. Many smaller nations, like Israel, had refused to aid Nebuchadnezzar in his war upon Arphaxad, and Nebuchadnezzar was determined to revenge himself upon these peoples, either by overcoming and ruling them or by taking every life of those who resisted him still.

At the head of Nebuchadnezzar's massive force was the merciless general, Holofernes, who had the confidence and friendship of the king himself and was recognized throughout the world as the face and voice of Nebuchadnezzar. By the time his unvanquished armies reached the borders of Israel, Holofernes was striking as much terror in the hearts of men as Nebuchadnezzar. As I mourned my husband and fasted, the pagan armies had rolled over the lands, and each nation had surrendered rather than fight such a formidable force.

In those days the high priest of Israel, Joakim, sent word to all our towns and cities that they must fortify themselves well for the fight to come, and hold strong because if the first Hebrew city could not be taken, then no city of Israel would fall. Yet, if the first city of Israel fell, so would all. Now it was known all over the world, wherever Israel was known, that if the Hebrew people were blameless before their God, no human force could take them because the Lord would fight on their side, and no army, no matter its size, could stand against him. It was also known that if the Hebrew people sinned against their God, he would not stand for them. Indeed, he had been known to punish them by causing them to be disbursed out of their land and made into exiles or slaves.

This was told to Holofernes, but in his arrogance, he doubted and disdained the power of God, saying that the Hebrews were a weak people whom he would easily defeat. And so, Holofernes marched with his great forces to the borders of Bethulia, and there took counsel with his generals and advisors. They told him that he could conquer my village without losing even one man to battle by simply taking control of the water springs that flowed from the foot of the nearby mountain. It was from these springs that all the people of Bethulia drew their water, they told the general, and without water and food they must either perish or surrender. Holofernes, approving this counsel, secured the springs and sent men to the tops of the surrounding mountains to ensure that no resident of Bethulia escaped, and that no other Hebrews came to our aid.

And suddenly all my village fasted with me.

But theirs was not a chosen fast, and they quickly grew weak and horrified as Holofernes and his army surrounded Bethulia, awaiting our fall. Children and women fainted away in the streets, and the oldest and infirm among the men soon joined them. But all this was as a distant drama to me, for I remained on my rooftop, communing only with the Lord and gaining strength through fasting and prayer. I was aware of the distress of Bethulia and its villagers, but I knew the power of God and expected the people to wait in trust. But, alas, they were not fortified with prayer and faith as I was, and so my solitude, perforce, was disturbed. When I learned that the villagers were clamoring for surrender to the pagan general after 34 days of this siege, I summoned Uzziah, the leader of our village, and the other elders. I did not go down into my house, nor put off my mourning, but told my most trusted maid to bring them up into my tent.

Uzziah and the elders had begged and finally convinced the people to hold strong for five more days, giving the Lord, our God, the opportunity to act. For this, I immediately chastised him. "What you have said to the people today is not right; you have even sworn and pronounced this oath between God and you, promising to surrender the town to our enemies unless the Lord turns and helps us within so many days," I remonstrated, "Who are you to put God to the test today, and to set yourselves up in the place of God in human affairs? You are putting the Lord Almighty to the test, but you will never learn anything! You cannot plumb the depths of the human heart or understand the workings of the human mind; how do you expect to search out God, who made all these things, and find out his mind or comprehend his thought?

"Therefore, while we wait for his deliverance, let us call upon him to help us, and he will hear our voice, if it pleases him…But we know no other god but him, and so we hope that he will not disdain us or any of our nation. For if we are captured, all of Judea will be captured and our sanctuary will be plundered; and he will make us pay for its desecration with our blood…For our slavery will not bring us into favor, but the Lord our God will turn it to dishonor."

With these and many other such words, I implored the leaders to remain fast and hold to the Lord, but in the end, Uzziah proved too weak to withstand the cries of the people. He replied, "But the people were so thirsty that they compelled us to do for them what we have promised, and made us take an oath that we cannot break. Now since you are a God-fearing woman, pray for us, so that the Lord may send us rain to fill our cisterns. Then we will no longer feel faint from thirst."

I knew then that these men were too weak to trust completely in God, and that I must act myself in the power of the Lord to protect our people and reveal the glory of the Lord. And so I dismissed these faint-hearted leaders with this prophecy, "Listen to me. I am about to do something that will go down through all generations of our descendants. Stand at the town gate tonight so that I may go out with my maid; and within the days after which you have promised to surrender the town to our enemies, the Lord will deliver Israel by my hand." Whether they believed me or not, I did not care. I simply wanted them gone now, out of my sight, and so they departed.

Once alone, I cast myself upon the ground in sackcloth and ashes, and cried out to the Lord, my God: "O God, my God, hear me also, a widow...Here now are the Assyrians, a greatly increased force, priding themselves in their horses and riders, boasting in the strength of their foot soldiers and trusting in shield and spear, in bow and sling. They do not know that you are the Lord who crushes wars; the Lord is your name. Break their strength by your might, and bring down their power in your anger; for they intend to defile your sanctuary, and to pollute the tabernacle where your glorious name resides...Give to me, a widow, the strong hand to do what I plan. By the deceit of my lips strike down the slave with the prince and the prince with his servant; crush their arrogance by the hand of a woman...Let your whole nation and every tribe know and understand that you are God, the God of all power and might, and that there is no other who protects the people of Israel but you alone!"

When I was finished with my prayer and adoration, I went down into my house and put off my garments of mourning.

I bathed and anointed myself in fine, aromatic oils. Recalling the days of joy with my husband Manasseh, I combed my hair and adorned it with a tiara, and then dressed myself festively as I had done in the days of our celebrating. I retrieved my jewels from the dark sack I had not opened in more than three years, and draped my arms and legs and neck and fingers and ears with anklets and bracelets and necklaces and rings until I virtually glimmered with gold and silver and the brilliant fire of precious jewels.

All the while my stomach heaved and twisted within me, protesting this betrayal of my husband and my grief, until I becalmed myself with faith: what I did, I did for my Lord and his nation. My stomach became like a smooth, cool stone within me. Still, I would not gaze upon myself in the glass, but when I summoned my loyal woman, I saw in her eyes that my appearance dazzled her. She was silent, as was her wont, but I knew I had made myself a temptation to all men. Such was my intention, but I took no pleasure in it.

I bade this maid to pack enough of our food to keep us for the prescribed time, and when she had, we went out to the gate of Bethulia where Uzziah and the others waited. They were stunned and not a little excited by my appearance, but I ignored them except to instruct, "Order that gate to be opened for me." I cared not that their eyes remained upon me until I'd passed from their sight.

Soon an Assyrian patrol met us, and they also were astounded, both by my presence there in their camp and by my beauty. The soldiers did as I requested, taking my woman and me to the tent of Holofernes. I heard their whispers about how the general would lust after me, and how they would thus be in great favor for bringing me to him. I closed my heart to these lewd murmurs and continued, allowing them to conduct us right to the very tent of Holofernes. This miserable, prideful man was reclining on a luxurious bed under a canopy woven with purple and gold and emeralds and every sort of precious stone.

It sickened me that he rested in such luxury while Israelites thirsted and starved, but when he came forward with his slaves carrying silver lamps, I cast him a limpid glance and after allowing him to fully gaze upon me, fell prostrate at his feet in a show of obeisance. His slaves immediately raised me up and I could hear the snickers of the soldiers who'd accompanied me as they saw the naked desire upon the face of their general.

Pretending to be faint, I waited until he'd urged me to take courage, and then I spoke, weaving ironical truth into the flattery and deceit I spoke in his ear, "Accept the words of your slave...I will say nothing false to my lord this night. If you follow the words of your servant, God will accomplish something through you, and my lord will not fail to achieve his purposes. For we have heard of your wisdom and skill, and it is reported throughout the whole world that you alone are the best in the whole kingdom, the most informed and the most astounding in military strategy."

As his ugly visage glowed under this false praise, I told him that I had fled my home in Bethulia because the Israelites had not been true to the Lord, the God of Israel, and that they planned to sin grievously against the Lord. When they did, I told Holofernes, echoing what he'd already been told, the Lord will allow them to "be handed over to you to be destroyed. So when I, your slave, learned all this, I fled from them. God has sent me to accomplish with you things that will astonish the whole world wherever people shall hear about them. Your servant is indeed God-fearing and serves the God of heaven night and day."

Not comprehending the truth that I spoke, Holofernes was mightily pleased by my words, and told me I would find succor and welcome in his camp. Then, I requested his permission to travel outside the camp daily to pray and purify myself before the Lord. He readily granted me this boon, and then, delighted with the opportunity to display his power over my comings and goings, he further agreed to let me eat and drink my own food with my own utensils so that I might not fall out of favor with the Lord my God. The puffed up fool, thinking to make me his permanent possession, asked me what would happen when my supply of food ran out.

Endeavoring not to laugh aloud at his fatal presumption, I answered demurely, "As surely as you live, my lord, your servant will not use up the supplies I have brought before the Lord carried out by my hand what he has determined."

For three days and nights, my woman and I remained in the Assyrian camp, availing ourselves of the permission Holofernes granted to come and go as we wished to pray and bathe. But my purpose in establishing this routine was more cunning, for on the fourth day, Holofernes sent his eunuch, Bagoas, to me to request my presence at a private banquet Holofernes intended to host that night. Of course this was no real invitation, for I had kept myself separate from Holofernes, knowing his lust to possess me would reach a crescendo. Knowing that I could not refuse, and indeed not wishing to, for his desire was in keeping with my avowed purpose, I agreed to attend the general at his private dinner.

Perhaps because I had made great show of my reticence, Holofernes did not invite any of his officers to this banquet, lest they shame me by witnessing my expected submission. This loutish attempt at sensitivity fell in perfectly with my plan, and thus the Lord again used the repulsive Holofernes to his glory.

When night came, I arrayed myself with much care so that I was more beautiful than before, if possible, when I entered Holofernes' tent and lay down to partake in the banquet. Though I ate and drank only what my maid had prepared, this did not dismay Holofernes in the least; he was besotted with me, and he himself drank an excessive amount of wine. By the time Bagoas, knowing his master's lust, had driven all the attendants away and closed the tent so that I might not slip away, Holofernes was insensible with drink. Soon he collapsed on his bed, and I was left alone with him.

I'd directed my woman to remain silently outside the great tent, for the Assyrians were accustomed to seeing us go to pray, and I wanted to arouse no suspicion. As she waited I observed the prone body of Holofernes and prayed in my heart: "O Lord God of all might, look in this hour on the work of my hands for the exaltation of Jerusalem. Now indeed is the time to help your heritage and to carry out my design to destroy the enemies who have risen up against us."

My heart beat slowly and steadily as I took Holofernes' mighty sword from its place. I returned to where he lay, and took a handful of his thick hair into my one hand. With the other I hefted the heavy sword and struck it down upon his neck with all my strength. The first blow did not sever his head, and so, without faltering, I struck again. His head came free from his body, which I then rolled from the bed onto the ground and pulled down the canopy. The head I took outside and gave to my woman, who put it in our food sack.

Having established the routine of leaving camp daily, we passed easily through Holofernes' guards and out of the camp. We hurried to the gate of Bethulia, and I called to sentries of Israel to open for us. Once inside the village, all the people gathered around us in astonishment while I called out in a loud voice, praising God. Then I took the sack and removed the head of our enemy, and the people cried out in astonishment and joy. I made certain to proclaim that I had maintained my purity, seducing Holofernes only with my face, and then Uzziah and the leaders glorified God and acclaimed me for my faith and courage.

But what could the approval of men mean to me, one approved by God?

I advised our people on how they might ensure the final victory over the leaderless Assyrians, and it came to pass according to my words. As soon as Bagoas summoned the courage—assuming, as he did, that I was with Holofernes and fearing to interrupt this ravaging—to enter his master's tent, he discovered the headless body and set up a cry throughout the camp of the Assyrians. Then those formerly brave soldiers, the best armies and infantries and chariots of Nebuchadnezzar, fled like frightened children before the wrath of the God of Israel. And following my teaching, Uzziah sent to all the border cities of Israel and they joined with the soldiers of Bethulia in pursuit of Nebuchadnezzar's force. Even those from Jerusalem and the hill country joined the hunt, and the Assyrians were cut down throughout all of Israel that day. Great booty and treasure was taken by our soldiers, and every town was enriched by the tremendous fall and slaughter of the enemy. I myself took possession of all the furnishings and trappings of Holofernes including the very canopy I had torn from his bed; I made of it a votive offering once we had been purified in Jerusalem. And I thought this just.

After thirty days of slaughter and plunder there was a great victory celebration, which I allowed myself to join for the glory of the name of the Lord. Joakim, the high priest of Israel, came to meet and bless me, and there was a great procession of dancing women whom I led, and we were followed by the men. I offered a great hymn of praise to the Lord, proclaiming and singing as had Deborah and Miriam and so many women of the Lord.

The Lord granted me a long life in that time, unto 105 years, and for all those years, no nation dared molest Israel. My name grew in renown and power, and I became the overseer of a great estate that combined my wealth with that of my husband. Many men would have wooed and married me, but I would have none of them. I had loved once and would not again. Nor would I give any man control over my property or my young men and women. I disbursed our riches as I wished among my kin and Manasseh's kin.

And I set free my maid, who had so faithfully followed me into the camp of Holofernes, and her loyalty remains ever in my heart.

Active Meditation

That Judith had courage is unquestionable. That she did gruesome violence in the name of the Lord is also unquestionable. From there on, we are left with nothing but questions! From the beginning of religious history, violence has been done, war has been waged, in the name of God. Or Yahweh. Or Allah. And too often, as we see in our world and indeed since the time of Jesus Christ, people claiming the same Creator, albeit with a different name, fight one another in his name!

How do we reconcile this? Who is right? Is it always just a matter of zealots who take religious writings/teachings to the extreme? Or are there situations when we should do violence in God's name? These are troubling and vital questions…questions too easily ignored in our day-to-day prayer and church life. But we do so at our spiritual—and perhaps, physical—peril.

Try to start or join a dialogue about these issues. If your congregation does not have a discussion program on today's religion-based conflicts, try to organize at least an initial discussion. If there is no interest—or approval—in your church, look for larger institutions—often ecumenical or educational—that sponsor such forums. Or, if you have like-minded friends or acquaintances, start a home discussion group. Such forums will not be easy, but only through communication and shared information can we at least begin to understand and resolve these conflicts.

Reflection/Discussion Questions

1. Does the prayer "God Bless America," mean "God make America,victorious" to you?

2. Under what circumstances is war, or violence, in the name of God, justified?

3. What is the difference between Judith's conviction and resulting action and those of a Palestinian woman who fights for her nation in the name of Allah?

4. Is there a difference between Islamic terrorists and those who claim to be members of extremist Christian groups like the Ku Klux Klan or the World Church?

5. How do you reconcile any war or violence with Jesus' life and message of love?

CHAPTER XI

Esther

Singular faith

ESTHER, CHAPTERS 1—10

For as long as I could remember, I had obeyed every word that came from the mouth of Mordecai. He was my cousin, much older than I, who had adopted me when my parents died. I was too young to even remember them, and Mordecai had been the only father I'd known. He'd treated me as his very own daughter, giving me discipline and love in equal measures and, above all, teaching me the ways and precepts of our people. I owed Mordecai my life and my respect; but my love he had earned, and I gave it as willingly as I would have given it to my parents. My cousin and adoptive father was a deeply pious Jew of the tribe of Benjamin, and his grandfather had been among the captives carried away from Jerusalem by King Nebuchadnezzar of Babylon.

A century later the Persians had vanquished the Babylonians, but we were still exiles, living hundreds of miles northeast of Jerusalem, in Susa, the city of the great pagan king of the Persians, Ahasuerus, who ruled the world. He was a brilliant leader, known for his fierce temper and political acumen, who ruled over 127 provinces from India to Ethiopia. The Jewish exiles had flourished throughout these provinces as we often did in foreign lands, and Mordecai was particularly well-regarded among the Jews in Susa. He made certain that I was raised in the Hebrew tradition, modest and well-schooled in the ways of the Lord, the God of Israel. So, having obeyed him all my life, I was devastated when he asked a new thing of me, a thing which seemed to deny all that he had taught me.

Mordecai told me I must accept—nay, court—the attentions of the greatest pagan in the world.

King Ahasuerus, in a fit of his famous temper, had banished his favorite queen, Vashti, from his royal presence because she had refused to attend him at a great banquet. On the advice of his counselors, the king proclaimed and undertook a search for a new queen, one who would obey him and indulge his every mood and wish. An edict went out that commissioners were to be appointed in each province to gather all the beautiful young virgins and bring them to the king's harem in Susa. From those gathered the king would choose the young virgin who most pleased him to be the next Queen of Persia.

When the order became known in Susa, Mordecai told me I would be among those gathered to the harem. I was horrified. All my dreams of a traditional marriage, in which I would come to my husband as a pious virgin ready to bear and raise our children, were destroyed. All my hopes of a life lived in the name of the Lord were dashed. While other Hebrew parents hid their daughters or sent them away to remote places where they might escape the attention of the king's commissioners, my beloved cousin told me I must submit to Ahasuerus' order. Though I would not refuse Mordecai, I implored him with many tears to explain how this could be. He would say only that this would be in God's hand and to advance the hopes of our people. He gave me only one instruction, and this too disturbed me greatly, more than anything that had yet happened.

"Tell no one in the palace that you are a Jew."

Desolate and confused, I approached the king's palace where I would be placed in the custody of Hegai, the eunuch whom the king had appointed to oversee all the virgins. The palace was like a vision, rising up and towering over other dwellings. It glimmered in the sun as though made of gold, and I soon discovered that parts of it were made of gold! It was also constructed of fine cedar and olive wood, replete with polished doors and marble pillars. A massive wall surrounded it to protect the king and the queen whom he would select and their many servants and advisors. It was as big as a city, and I was paralyzed with fear at the entrance. I could not make my feet move, and as I stood still, certain I would be killed for refusing to enter the palace gates, I remembered what Mordecai had taught me so many years ago.

I had been a painfully shy child, fearful of speaking or drawing attention because I knew I was different from other girls who had parents. I could barely speak at all, never mind to defend or explain myself. Once, when I had run home to Mordecai crying because some other children had teased me, he had taken me in his arms and told me, "My little daughter, there is nothing amiss in silence. The Lord blesses the quiet, pious girl who grows up to be the soft-speaking, obedient woman. So, you see, you are already much wiser than those rude children who know not the will of the Lord. But you must not run from them. Neither must you answer them with many foolish words. You will answer them with your bearing and your posture. You will answer them by holding your head high, knowing that you are beloved of God. You will answer them by the soft smile on your face which you will wear for the eyes of the Lord and no other. You will answer them in this manner, and to these things, they will have no retort."

And this is what I did, silencing my enemies and demonstrating by my demeanor that I was a faithful child of the Lord. As I grew into womanhood, my silence and my bearing earned me much respect, for I never spoke more than was necessary and thus, no foolish word passed my lips.

But I never knew, as Mordecai did, that I was greatly admired for my beauty as well, and this was enhanced by my reputation for wisdom.

And so I entered the great gates and went into the palace, remembering those lessons learned so long ago. Never had I seen such wealth. Precious gems and gold were everywhere. The floor was marble, covered with intricate designs and mosaics. Every table held vessels of gold and silver. Vibrantly colored draperies tied with silk cords hung from the ceiling and marble pillars. Low couches covered with velvet were trimmed with pearls. I was conducted along the way by Hegai himself, and though I could not know it, he was impressed by my dignity and silence. Indeed, I later learned he was relieved for he had spent his days and nights trying to cope with the demands and tears and cries of hundreds of virgins from every province. My seeming calmness was a welcome respite, and perhaps to show me favor, he stopped by one large chamber protected by gold and silver chains and said, "This is the court where the king conducts business and hears petitions. No one may enter unless the king lifts his scepter in welcome. Anyone who enters without this sign from the king will immediately be put to death. Remember this, Esther!"

I was far from comforted. How could any woman desire a husband as cruel as King Ahasuerus? But I could not ask Hegai such a question, and I composed myself to follow him. Soon, we arrived at the quarters which Hegai had selected for me; chambers filled with large silver urns holding peacock feathers and other beautiful ornamentation. Thousands of candles lit the rooms. In the center of one was a bed nearly as big as my room at home, partially concealed by a canopy flowing with violet silk. Heavy scarlet curtains hung from the ceiling to the floor, covering the walls, and there were couches with soft pillows. But all this was as nothing to me. I would have traded it in an instant for sackcloth and ashes if I could have been back in my little home with Mordecai. Hegai again favored me, though I was too distraught to understand, providing me with the finest cosmetics and adornments and leaving seven maids to attend me. I disguised my astonishment and thanked him quietly.

Hegai did not forget me. He allowed Mordecai to ask after me each day, and he instructed the gate-keepers to assure my cousin of my welfare. According to the king's edict, each virgin must remain in the harem for twelve months before she could be presented to the king, and when the requisite time had passed, Hegai came to me again. When he inquired what I needed to prepare to go before the king, I softly told him I would accept whatever he suggested. A bright flush of approval rose in his face, and he himself took charge of my anointing and adornment. Using his own unerring instinct for the king's desire, Hegai dressed me simply with few jewels or other ornaments. He allowed my maids to apply only a light touch of myrrh and oil to my skin, and then I was led away to appear before King Ahasuerus.

Hegai knew well what he was doing, though I did not, for when I entered into the king's presence, he found himself looking upon the most beautiful woman he'd ever seen. Immediately he was smitten with me and proclaimed that I was to be his queen. When Hegai, rejoicing, brought me the news, my heart sank. Was this truly what Mordecai had intended? That I be given to a pagan who seemed to care little for the Lord, God of Israel? That I be wife in body, mind, and spirit to such a man? And, if so, why was I to conceal from him and all his people that I was an Israelite? I longed to ask Mordecai these questions that so plagued me, but I would have no opportunity. When Hegai left, gleeful in the triumph he presumed we shared, I felt I had reached the most desperate point in my life. But I kept my face clear and my head high as the inner turmoil raged. I could only keep repeating to myself Mordecai's assurance that the sacrifice of my piety and virginity to the Persian king was for the greater good of our people.

And I became the king's wife.

I suppose my life must have been every woman's dream. At least, every woman in my time. Though the king was fearsome in temperament, he loved me as deeply as such a man can and provided me with every honor imaginable. Banquets, festivals, and holidays were declared in my name. I had everything I could have wished for, and many things I did not care about at all. Jewels. Garments. Veils. Crowns. Riches beyond compare. Every delicacy that existed for food. More servants than I could count or ever truly need. I could not have imagined such bounty, and in my life as queen, it became commonplace. Throughout all this, I kept my own counsel, trusting only Hathach, the chief eunuch whom Hegai had appointed to serve me. It was through him alone that I continued to communicate with Mordecai. And as I'd promised, I never revealed to the king that I was a Jew.

But it was a Jew who saved the life of my husband. A man as strong and renowned, not to mention fierce and sometimes cruel, as Ahasuerus had many enemies. The most dangerous ones were in his own court. One day when Mordecai was lingering outside the palace gates to learn news of me, he overheard two of the king's eunuchs, Bigthan and Teresh, speaking angrily of the king. They described their plan to assassinate him within his own chambers, and when Mordecai had fully ascertained the details of their plot, he sent word to me. The plan was imminent, and I quickly sent word to my husband, who received the warning just in time. When the rebels came to attack him, his strongest soldiers were waiting. Bigthan and Teresh were hanged on the gallows before night fell.

When Ahasuerus asked how I'd learned of the plot, I replied that Mordecai, the Jew, had sent word to save the king, but I did not say that Mordecai was my cousin and father. My husband, in a particularly expansive and grateful mood, decreed that the story of Mordecai's loyalty be written in the book of annals of the kingdom. Though this was an extraordinary honor—particularly for a Jew—I somehow knew that personal gain had not been Mordecai's objective.

Weeks passed in relative quiet. My husband had not sent for me in thirty days, but I knew he was occupied with his massive kingdom, and I was relieved for the respite. One morning one of my maids awakened me with dire and confusing tidings. "My queen!" she cried, "A terrible thing has happened! Mordecai the Jew is outside the palace walls, dressed in sackcloth, wailing and covering his head with ashes! He will not be moved and he resists the king's soldiers!"

I swiftly sent Hathach to bring Mordecai in to me, but my cousin refused, replying for all to hear that he would not enter the king's home! Greatly agitated, I sent Hathach back to ask Mordecai for some explanation. Pale and trembling, Hathach returned with Mordecai's terrible and astonishing answer: the king, my husband, had ordered the execution of every Jew in his kingdom's 127 provinces! Ahasuerus had acted so barbarically because he'd been deceived by his chief advisor, Haman. Haman hated Mordecai because my cousin refused to kneel before him in the manner of all other subjects of the king. Haman craved this honor, but Mordecai would kneel only before the Lord our God, and no man—not even the powerful Haman—could bring my cousin to his knees. Haman was so enraged at this that he paid a great deal of money into the king's treasury and then cajoled my husband into commanding death for all Jews! The proclamations were to go out to every province.

Hathach, his face now covered with tears, concluded with Mordecai's instruction to me, "He says you must go in to the king's court and beg him to spare your people."

Terrified, I sent word back to Mordecai, "All the king's servants and the people of the king's provinces know that if any man or woman goes to the king inside the inner court without being called, there is but one law—all alike are to be put to death."

Mordecai, my beloved Mordecai, was unmoved and he sent a grim message back to me, "Do not think you will escape any more than all the other Jews. For if you keep silence at such a time as this, relief and deliverance will rise for the Jews from another quarter, but you and your father's family will perish. Perhaps you have come to royal dignity for just such a time as this."

I thought to myself, better say, "I have sold you into royal dignity for just such a time as this," when Mordecai's words were repeated to me. For that is what my cousin had done. But I would not disobey him after all this time; it was not in my nature. So I sent word to Mordecai that all of the Jews in the world must pray and fast for me for three days and three nights, and I would do the same as preparation. "After that, I will go to the king, though it is against the law, and if I perish, I perish."

Then, I tore away my royal raiment and cast down my jewels. I clothed myself in rough garments and covered my head with ashes, praying and fasting for three days and nights before the Lord, my God. My prayers always began thus, "O my Lord, you only are our King; help me, who am alone and have no helper but you, for danger is in my hand." And after many pleas and lamentations, I ended my words to the Lord, "Your servant has had no joy since the day that I was brought here until now, except in you, O Lord God of Abraham. O God, whose might is over all, hear the voice of the despairing, and save us from the hands of evildoers. And save me from my fear."

After that, I put off my rags and ashes.

I called my most trusted maid and bid them dress and adorn me in the richest possible array. My most sparkling gems, the most intricately worked gold, translucent veils, my daintiest slippers. Nothing was spared. Beads and silver were worked into my hair in elaborate braids and weaves so that my loveliest crown was but a pretty addition. Perfumes and ointments that I had never before used were smoothed into my skin, and the darkest kohl framed my eyes.

Thus, I prepared to enter the king's court. While my demeanor remained calm, my heart quaked. Ahasuerus might well become furious, and if he did not raise his scepter to me immediately, I would be put to death! And all my people with me if I failed. All this passed through my mind as my maids, full of excitement for they did not know my intention, adorned me. I could tell by their faces that I virtually shimmered with splendor and beauty. I was ready to go. But was I going to my death?

Faint and leaning heavily upon my two maids, I walked slowly until I finally stood at the entrance to the king's court. Trembling, the color drained from my face until my eyes were like burning jewels set in the moon. Remembering the Lord, my God, I lifted my head and walked into the chamber.

Enraged at the interruption, Ahasuerus looked up to see who dared enter. When I saw his fury, my heart failed me and I began to swoon. But before I fell to the floor, my husband leapt from his throne and caught me in his arms. Then, swiftly recalling his own rule, he grasped his scepter and raised it to show all that Esther was welcome and not subject to death. Ignoring all those in the court, he spoke softly to me, "My wife, what troubles you? Share with me the burden weighing your heart."

I could barely find my voice, but knowing I must try to save my people, I whispered, "My king, come to feast with me in my chambers tonight with your chief advisor, Haman, and I will unburden myself to you then." My husband readily agreed, and when I'd returned to my rooms, Haman was summoned and told that he was being greatly honored by an invitation to dine that very night with the king and queen. Filled with proud pleasure, he immediately told everyone from his wife and servants to his neighbors and soldiers about this extraordinary honor. Preening mightily, he proceeded through the streets so that all may know of his good fortune and pay him obeisance.

Despite this, Haman was infuriated to see Mordecai sitting in the dirt outside the palace. Even if the entire world honored Haman, he would not be happy unless Mordecai kneeled before him! Still Mordecai would not, and immediately, Haman's pleasure was dissipated. He raged and complained to all who would listen of Mordecai's insolence until finally Haman's wife and counselors advised him to have Mordecai put to death. Pleased at this counsel, Haman told his soldiers to build a gibbet upon which Mordecai would soon be hanged. After delivering this command, he bathed and dressed with much care and, well pleased with himself, went to the banquet.

I received my husband and Haman graciously. As we ate, the king again mentioned the anxiety he had seen in me earlier that day, and he asked me to tell him what had disturbed my peace. Instead of answering him directly, I said, "My husband, you appear weary. Have you been sleeping well?"

"No, my wife," he replied, "I've been plagued by sleeplessness. Have you any advice?"

"Perhaps you might pass your sleepless hours reading the book of annals of your kingdom. It contains many worthy stories," I suggested, knowing that the book told how Mordecai had saved the king.

After accepting this advice, he insisted that I tell him what had troubled me. But I merely cast my eyes down and said, "If I have won the king's favor, and if it pleases the king to grant my petition and fulfill my request, let the king and Haman come tomorrow to the banquet that I will prepare for them, and then I will do as the king has said."

"I will," he answered with an astonishing show of patience, and soon after, he and Haman departed. Puffed up with pride at being the only guest at the royal banquet, Haman accompanied Ahasuerus to his rooms. There, the king took my advice and opened the annals of the kingdom. After reading about how Mordecai had saved him from the plot of his evil stewards, he remembered that Mordecai had never been rewarded. The king asked Haman, "What shall be done for the man whom the king wishes to honor?"

Thinking the king meant him, Haman answered, "Let royal robes be brought, which the king has worn, and a horse that the king has ridden, with a royal crown on its head. Let the robes and the horse be handed over to one of the king's most noble officials; let him robe the man whom the king wishes to honor, and let him conduct the man on horseback, through the open square of the city, proclaiming before him: 'Thus shall it be done for the man whom the king wishes to honor.'"

Haman thought Ahasuerus would order all this for him, but instead the king said, "Quickly, take the robes and the horse, as you have said, and do so to Mordecai who sits at the king's gate. Leave out nothing that you have mentioned."

Haman was mortified. He was to honor the very man he planned to hang! Haman could not bear to think of himself leading Mordecai around the city on the king's horse, but he dared not disobey. The next day, shamed and humiliated, he dressed Mordecai in the king's purple cloak, crowned him with the king's gold crown, and led him around the city on the king's best horse. Mordecai held himself tall so as to give hope and pride to every Jew who saw him.

When Haman returned from his humiliating task of honoring Mordecai, he found the king's eunuchs waiting to escort him to my second banquet. Though greatly humbled and dismayed, he knew he must go, and when he arrived, the king was already at my table. But Haman was not to eat of this second feast.

Before the first course had been served the king again asked me, "What is your petition, Queen Esther? It shall be granted to you."

I answered, "If I have won your favor, O king, and if it pleases the king, let my life be given me and the lives of my people—that is my request. For we have been sold, I and my people, to be destroyed, to be killed and to be annihilated."

Astonished, Ahasuerus demanded, "Who is he, and where is he, who has presumed to do this?"

Pointing, I cried, "A foe and enemy, this wicked Haman!"

Enraged beyond words, my husband strode out into the palace garden to recover his temper. Haman, terrified, threw himself on the couch where I reclined to beg my mercy. But my husband returning at that very moment to see Haman clutching at me where I lay, was even more infuriated. One of the eunuchs attending us at the feast—having little love for the arrogant Haman—told the king, "Look, the very gallows that Haman has prepared for Mordecai, whose word saved the king, stands at Haman's house." Immediately, Ahasuerus ordered that Haman be hanged on the same gibbet he'd built for my cousin Mordecai.

I then told my husband all that had been plotted against the Jews, of whom I was one, and I told him of my relationship with Mordecai. The king ordered that all Haman's household and goods be given to me, and I, in turn, set Mordecai over all Haman's property. After also honoring Mordecai and giving him great power throughout the kingdom, my husband rescinded his previous command. He sent letters to all 127 provinces in his empire freeing all Jews from the decree of death and ordering that they be revered throughout the kingdom. From that day on, my people had a special holiday called Purim celebrating their triumph over their enemies throughout the world.

Some credit my husband for inaugurating this holiday. Some pay this honor to me. Still others say it was Mordecai who gave us this festival. But I know that it was the Lord, my God, he who helped me, who was alone and had no helper but him.

Active Meditation

"O my Lord, help me, who am alone and have no helper but you." This short plea, uttered when Esther was completely alone and torn by competing loyalties, is one of the most moving prayers in Scripture. Have we felt so completely alone, so seemingly abandoned, even as those we love or need demand action from us? Have we felt so uncertain of our own strength? How about when our oncologist recommends a radical mastectomy while friends urge a less invasive course? Or when our child's counselor suggests a residential treatment center while the child begs for one more chance? Or when our spouse seeks a job across the country while our aging parents want us nearby?

Life is full—too full—of times when all the considerable and sobering responsibilities of a situation rest on us. Or seem to. The next time you face such a time, remember Esther's prayer; indeed, her solution. Find a quiet place, make yourself comfortable, close your eyes, and imagine God with you. Only God, surrounding you, comforting you, counseling you, loving you, lifting the burden from you. Say: "O my Lord, help me, who am alone and have no helper but you." Allow yourself to feel, savor, God's presence. Allow the certainty that you are not alone because he is with you to flow through you like cool water.

Become familiar with how it feels to have God, and God alone, on your side, by your side. Carry this sense, this vision, with you into your life. Don't hesitate to seek it again—whether in a crowded room or lying in bed wishing for sleep—as you address the difficult issues in your life.

Reflection/Discussion Questions

1. Have you ever carried a burden that made you feel completely alone?
2. In difficult times is your first impulse to seek God or rely on your own coping skills?
3. When you seek advice, is it important that the advisor, doctor, friend or other have faith?
4. How do you feel about the Christian Science philosophy that God is the only healer, and therefore, medical intervention is to be avoided?
5. If you were speaking to someone who had no faith, how would you describe yours?

CHAPTER XII

Susanna

Purity of spirit and body

DANIEL, CHAPTER 13

Before that grievous, hot summer afternoon, I would have said I was the happiest woman in the world.

I would have been wrong.

Oh, I surely had everything a pious woman of my day could have possibly wanted. My husband, Joakim, was a well-respected Jew and wealthy resident of Babylon where we lived in a gorgeous home adjoining spacious gardens. My parents and family were always welcome in our home, for my father, Hilkiah, had raised me strictly in the law of Moses. We were of the tribe of Judah, and Joakim had been pleased to get a wife who fitted so well in his world. I was also said to have great beauty.

Joakim saw to it that I had every possession and accoutrement appropriate for a wife of his. No expense was spared on my garments or jewelry. I anointed myself with the finest oils and perfumes, and I had a cadre of maids waiting to hear my every wish. My children were loving and obedient, and I ensured that they were raised according to the word of the Lord. I saw to it that they brought my husband nothing but honor. It was important, too, that I appear wise and lovely and modest in the

eyes of Joakim's colleagues, for he was an important man, and many
Jews came to him for advice and social intercourse. Indeed, two elders of
our people—two men who had been elected judges—regularly held their
court in my husband's home. Almost every day these two old and revered
men would come, and the people would appear before them to try their
cases. Of course, this only increased the esteem in which Joakim was
held by the entire community, and my father never ceased to congratu-
late himself on having made me such a good marriage.

Well aware of my position, it was my habit to remain indoors and
busy about household affairs while the elders held court in my husband's chambers. I did not want to seem immodest or to parade myself
before the community of men that met in our home. Only after they
dispersed, usually at noon, would I walk freely with my maids in our
lovely gardens. I had, from the beginning of my marriage, treated my
young women well. I knew that many wealthy woman did not deign to
pay attention to their servants, and some even allowed the worst kind
of abuses to occur in their households. But I would not countenance
such things, and my maids learned that they could depend upon me.

Besides, I was often lonely and enjoyed both their company and their
loyalty.

We conversed easily during our sojourns in the garden, and I learned
much about their families and their lives and their hopes. I encouraged
them to speak freely, and thus, discovered much about the world outside our gates since they ventured forward into the world much more
frequently than I. The maid who had been with me the longest, Bethala,
was particularly fearless in speaking her mind, until one afternoon
when I thought she went too far.

We were strolling, as was our wont, through the carefully maintained
paths, and I had not yet paused to bathe and cool myself in the garden
pool. Bethala was carrying on a lively conversation with the others
when I heard her voice take on a telltale huskiness. "Speak up," I told
her, laughing, "Surely you have nothing to say that is not worthy of my
ears!" Bethala gave me a swift look, and then said with more reluctance
than was characteristic, "Only this, mistress: I was saying that the two
elders who come always to the master's chambers to so righteously

judge the people may find themselves being judged some day before the Lord!"

This was not typical of her usual lighthearted, if somewhat barbed, chatter, and I turned my full attention upon her. Noticing that the other maids had grown silent and somber, I spoke more seriously, "Bethala, what do you mean to say? These are respected men in our community."

She heard the warning in my voice, but her jaw took on a familiar stubborn set, and after a brief moment, she muttered, "Respected, perchance, by those who do not know the truth that I know!"

Losing patience, as I seldom did, I commanded sternly, "Tell us this truth, then, Bethala, or leave off speaking such nonsense."

Instead of retreating as I thought she would, she raised her eyes defiantly to mine, and retorted, "The truth about those judges whom our master entertains is that they force their unwanted attentions upon innocent and defenseless women, threatening to accuse and judge any woman who refuses to lie with them."

I made no reply at first, stunned by Bethala's words. I did not even consider that they might be true; rather, I was appalled that she would repeat such malicious falsehoods. No doubt the two judges had aroused the jealousy of some gossip-mongers, and so, such ridiculous accusations had been falsely spread through the servants. I knew that Joakim was occasionally the subject of such prevarication because he too was renowned, and thus, inspired the envy of ill-minded folk. I dismissed Bethala's ludicrous words without a second thought, admonishing her soberly, "I will not hear such vicious speech in my home. You should know better, Bethala! You, of all my women, know how often ill is said of your master, rising our of envious hearts and mouths. And it is all false. How can you repeat such things about other respected men? I am disappointed in you."

Bethala said nothing more, and my other maids fell into distressed silence, for they were not accustomed to harsh words from me. But Bethala, who usually recovered her happy disposition in no time at all, even after being chastised, sent me sidelong glances as we continued our walk. Indeed, the afternoon was ruined, and we returned to the house shortly thereafter. I did not even bathe in the garden pool, as was my habit on warm summer days. I said nothing of Bethala's gossip to my husband; Joakim was much more stern with our young men and women, and I did not wish him to dismiss Bethala in outrage, as I knew he would, for such impertinence.

The days passed slowly, and the good relations between myself and my maids were soon restored, although I noticed that none of them wished to wait upon my husband and the elders when they convened. I did not press the matter, nor did Bethala and I speak of it again. But whenever I was summoned into the presence of the men and my husband, Bethala insisted upon accompanying me as if she would protect me from some evil. I considered talking to her about this, but decided not to as I did not wish to create another rift between us.

That season was long and hot, and I frequently asked my maids to close the garden gates in the afternoon so that I might bathe in the heat of the day. One such afternoon, I went forward into the gardens after the elders and the people had departed at noon for lunch. There was much work to be done in the household that day since we were to soon have guests, so I took only Bethala and another of my young women with me. After we'd walked for some short time, I sent them back for olive oil and ointments so that I might bathe and anoint myself. They brought them back and would have attended me, but I bade them return to the house and help with preparations while I bathed alone. The youngest immediately obeyed me, but Bethala was loath to go. Looking closely around the vast gardens, she asked if she might stay nearby while I bathed. Smiling, I told her, "You will not escape your work so easily! Go back now, and close the gates behind you so that no one may enter. I will be with you shortly."

Still she hesitated, but I insisted, and after she'd gone, I shed my robe and stepped into the cool water. Immediately I heard a rustling, and looking up in horror, I saw the two elders who had only pretended to depart for lunch. Instead, they'd hidden themselves carefully in the garden, knowing full well that I was wont to bathe there on hot afternoons. I clutched my robe to me, but to little avail. Leering at me, they spoke evilly, telling me that I must lie with them, or they would raise a cry and accuse me publicly. If I refused or called for help, they would claim that they had found me lying with a lover, and they would see me tried for adultery. The punishment would, of course, be death. And that was nothing to the shame I would feel before my husband and family and neighbors, all of whom thought me blameless and pious in the eyes of God.

Despairing, I suddenly realized that every word Bethala had spoken was true. I now knew that she had meant to warn me, and I'd given her nothing but a scolding for her love and loyalty. Nonetheless, there was no question about what I must do, and so I told the two wretched men, "If I do this, it will mean death for me; if I do not, I cannot escape your hands. I choose not to do it; I will fall into your hands, rather than sin in the sight of the Lord." And then I cried out for rescue.

But they shouted the louder, and when Joakim with all the people and servants in our house rushed into the garden, the words of those lechers prevailed, for they were men revered in Israel. I saw shame and anguish in the face of my husband, but he spoke no word in my defense. Our servants cried out in sorrow together, as if with one voice, but Bethala's eyes simmered with rage as she fixed them upon the two old men.

My trial was held the next day. My parents, mourning and fearful, attended me, as did my children and all my relatives when I was summoned before the court held in my husband's chambers. In all the days that this court had convened in my home, I had never imagined I would come before it in such a manner. When I entered, the room was filled with people. Joakim was also present, but he did not raise his eyes to meet mine; nor did he speak. He had not come to comfort me the night before, and indeed, I'd not seen him since I'd been so cruelly accused. Bethala supported me as I walked into the midst of the room. She had covered my face with a veil, so as to provide me some respite from staring faces and to preserve what modesty I still possessed.

But the two old sinners would not have this, and they immediately demanded that my face be uncovered. When the veil was ripped away and those two put their filthy hands upon my head, all my maids and my family wept. But their weeping was nothing next to the agony that rent me as I felt those gnarled, grasping hands upon me while those rheumy eyes greedily drank in my ravaged beauty. I felt as if they would take today what I had refused them yesterday; bile flooded my throat and my skin crawled as if covered with insects. That my children and my parents should witness this was more than I could bear, and I could feel tears on my exposed face.

But just when desolation touched the very center of my being, I remembered the Lord, and putting my trust in him, I lifted my face to heaven. There I kept my needful attention while the two lechers accused me, as they'd promised, of lying with a lover in my husband's gardens. The assembly, as naturally it would, believed these men they thought to be good and pious judges of Israel; I was condemned to die.

Then, heedless of those around me, I lifted my voice to the Lord, "O eternal God, you know what is secret and are aware of all things before they come to be; you know that these men have given false evidence against me. And now I am to die, though I have done none of the wicked things that they have charged against me!"

The Lord, my God, heard my plea, for as I was being led away to execution, I saw Bethala hurrying to the midst of the assembly, accompanied by a tall, handsome youth. She stopped, not daring to step forward herself, but she gestured toward him as he shouted in a loud voice, "I want no part in shedding this woman's blood! Are you such fools, O Israelites, as to condemn a daughter of Israel without examination and without learning the facts? Return to court, for these men have given false evidence against her."

This boy, Daniel, was filled with the Holy Spirit of the Lord, and the people listened to him; for, indeed, many were loath to see me executed and did not wish to believe what had been said of me. So they readily agreed when Daniel asked that they return to court and allow him to examine the two elders. Before those two could confer and plot together, Daniel insisted they be separated so that he might examine them one at a time. Knowing the cruel lust that possessed them both—for Bethala had indeed been right, and Daniel also knew how they'd exploited other women through their connivance and power—Daniel called the first to come before him and all the assembly.

Now both men had testified falsely that they had seen me lying with a lover under a tree in the garden, and so, chiding the first old man for his lust and abuse of women, Daniel asked one question only: what tree had he seen us under? "Under a mastic tree," came the answer, though the evil elder was much diminished in voice and demeanor when he heard the question. Daniel then sent for the second judge and after also condemning him for his behavior, asked the same question. This man, looking around nervously as though someone might supply the correct answer, finally answered in a barely discernible voice, "An oak tree."

At this a great cry went up from the people for I had been vindicated! Indeed, my husband's gardens boasted both oak trees and mastic trees, but they could not be easily confused: the mastic was a small and delicate tree, while the sturdy oak towered high above all others. According to the law of Moses, the two elders, corrupted by perversion and lust, were led off to the death they had sought for me. I might have spoken for them, but never had I been an obstacle to the law; nor would I start now.

Family and friends surrounded me, babbling with joy. My parents carried on loudly, giving thanks to God, blessing him and proclaiming my purity and innocence. But their voices were not as pleasing to my ears as they had been before. My husband embraced me with great fervor, but his embrace did not awaken comfort and joy in me as it had before. My neighbors sang of my virtues, but their praise did not sound as lovely as it had before.

Bethala, before hurrying in to prepare a feast for the crowd, swiftly slipped her hand into mine and gripped it warmly, and her touch was as true and sweet as ever it had been.

It is true that I thought myself happy before these days of travesty. But I learned that happiness was not to be found in possessions or husband or family or status. None of these could help me when I most needed aid. They amounted to nothing next to the Lord, my true help. My only help. And only after he used my plight to reveal his strength and splendor did I know the meaning of happiness and fulfillment.

Active Meditation

Susanna may seem a little incredible to us today. As we imagine her pressing her hand, palm outward, against her brow and all but moaning, "Woe is me," we may be tempted to shake her by the shoulders and demand, "Stand up for yourself, woman! Where's your backbone?"

And yet, Susanna is the perfect illustration of Paul's claim that God manifests his strength in our weakness. Do we surrender our weakness to God so that he may show his strength? Or rather, in these modern times when independence is so revered, do we grit our teeth and vow to be strong no matter how difficult the adversity we face? Are we committed to "handle it" lest we display any sign of weakness or vulnerability?

Recall a situation in your life when you were determined to "be strong" in addressing a difficult issue. Now imagine what might have happened had you allowed yourself to be weak and vulnerable. Resist the urge to dismiss even the possibility of a different, positive outcome. Might your weakness or surrender have given God the chance to demonstrate his power? For example, if you showed the world you could "handle" every aspect of a loved one's—or your own—serious illness, might you have denied God the opportunity to show the world his strength through the loving help of friends or acquaintances? If you fought your way to a promotion you were determined to have, might you have prevented God from showing his love by leading you to a more positive job opportunity?

Promise yourself you will "consider weakness" in the future so as to allow God to reveal his strength.

Reflection/Discussion Questions

1. Can weakness ever be a virtue in our competitive, independent-minded society?
2. Can you name an example where God has "shown his strength" in weakness?
3. Is it easier for a man or a woman to reveal weakness or vulnerability in our world?
4. Do you think that God demonstrates his power through others in your life?
5. Might your need to "prove" yourself strong ever have cost you an opportunity to receive God's strength and grace?